ORDER
in the COURTS

BRINGING BALANCE & UNDERSTANDING
IN EXPRESSIVE PRAISE & WORSHIP

D1213427

PAUL WILBUR

ORDER IN THE COURTS.
Copyright © 2007 by Paul Wilbur.
First Edition

Wilbur Ministries
10920-27 Baymeadows Road
Suite 127
Jacksonville, FL 32256
www.wilburministries.com

Cover Photography: Stefan Klein
Artwork by Ismael Burciaga, Church Media Group, Inc., www.churchmedia.cc

This book is dedicated to my wife, Luanne, who has served at my side for nearly thirty years, and to my two sons Nathan and Joel. You never complained about the untold hours of separation and sacrifice while I traversed the globe to fulfill the commission given to us all, way back when bell-bottom jeans were in fashion for the very first time!

Luanne, you are my counsel and friend and a much better example of what it means to be a disciple than I could ever hope to be. Thank you sweetheart for trusting the Lord and choosing me for this lifelong walk; I know the Lord is pleased with you and I am forever grateful.

To Nathan and Joel, the olive shoots around my table, the arrows of my quiver and the joy of my life. Thank you both for loving the Lord enough to sow your father into the harvest of Israel and the nations; you guys are awesome!

Paul Wilbur, husband and father.

CONTENTS

FOREWORD

I remember distinctly the first worship service I was in that was led by Paul Wilbur. It was March 30, 1985, at a messianic congregation in Maryland where I was scheduled to speak. Many of the messianic Jewish elements were new to me, despite my being a Jewish believer, and I was not sure how I felt about all of the "messianic frills."

My wife, Nancy, and I were in the front row, and the moment the worship began we *instantly* sensed the presence of the Lord in a wonderful, powerful way, looking at each other with tears in our eyes, not needing to say a word. Immediately, we knew two things: The Lord was in this place, and His hand was on the worship team. Even as I write these words, I remember the reality of that glorious presence. There is no substitute for the holy anointing of God!

A few years later, I became part of the leadership team in that same congregation, serving alongside Paul. On occasion, Paul would bring his guitar to a leadership team meeting and would begin to worship as we started our time of prayer. That was it! We would quickly get caught up in the presence of the Lord and the agenda would have to be scrapped. To this day, more than twenty years later, I eagerly anticipate being in a worship service led by Paul Wilbur, and I can think of no one better equipped to write this important little book. As the saying goes, he knows whereof he speaks!

Here are some of the reasons why you should read and digest this book very carefully, especially if you are a pastor or worship leader.

First, Paul is a serious worshiper of God. Now, if you get to know him, you'll see at once that he is a fun-loving guy – in fact, you'll figure that out by just reading this book – but for him, worship is not just fun and games, and it is certainly not a performance. It is a holy, often joyous time of coming before the King of kings, and Paul has been used by the Lord to help restore reverence in our worship, something that has been sadly lacking in many of our Pentecostal and Charismatic circles.

Second, Paul is a man of the Word. He is an extraordinarily gifted singer, songwriter, and musician (for those wondering, he did *not* pay me to say that), but he is also a student of the Scriptures who has dug into the Word for several decades. What does the Word say about worship and praise? How can order and freedom go hand in hand? What can we learn from the biblical patterns? These are all issues that are addressed in the pages that follow, with frequent recourse to the Scriptures.

Third, Paul has been exposed to a *wide* variety of worship styles, from the Jewish dances of the Messianic Movement to tribal expressions in Africa, and from liturgical services to Holy Ghost explosions. And if you have been in any of his services, you will witness a tremendous amount of liberty and exuberance and freedom. At the same time, you will soon realize that not everything goes, and that there is a time to shout and a time to be silent. Paul has consistently evidenced a strong sensitivity to the Spirit, and he brings that sensitivity and experience to the pages that follow.

To be sure, some people will be offended by what he writes, feeling restricted or hindered or quenched. But there are some things that *should* be restricted and hindered and quenched, and Paul gives sound reasons for the order that he advocates. Bluntly stated, it's not about you (or me), it's about the Lord and His corporate body, and if our hearts are set on honoring Him and considering one another, our worship will be all the more powerful.

Sometimes truth hurts, and some of our worship habits do need pruning. But the end result of divine pruning will be greater and more glorious fruit along with a deeper, more wonderful presence of the Lord. And if we allow our petty, personal liberties to be subjected to the greater good, we will experience the real liberty of the Spirit, where Yeshua is mightily exalted.

So, dive in and enjoy these wise, worship gems from a master teacher, and then go and worship the King.

Dr. Michael L. Brown
President, FIRE School of Ministry
Concord, NC
www.revolutionnow.org

PREFACE

For more than three decades, I have led praise and worship as a cantor, associate pastor, worship leader, and recording artist. I have had the distinct privilege of working with some of the leading Christian ministers and ministries of the 20th century including Pat Robertson, Jack Hayford, John Hagee, Benny Hinn, Kenneth Copeland and others, as well as helping to establish the worship and work of the international Messianic Jewish movement.

I began my walk with the Lord as a founding member of the contemporary Christian singing group "Harvest." It was there in Bloomington, Indiana, that I met Jerry Williams, the young man who would eventually lead me to the Lord in March of 1977. We traveled and ministered together for over four years, and recorded several albums with Benson Records in Nashville, Tennessee. It has been my honor to serve as Cantor/Worship leader for ten years at Beth Messiah Congregation with Dr. Daniel Juster as well as Associate Pastor/Worship Leader for five years at Midwest Christian Center in Chicago alongside Pastor Robb Thompson. I have been a recording artist on three major record labels including Benson Records, Maranatha! Records, and for the past two decades with Integrity Media. I have also had the joy of ministering in over fifty nations, on almost every continent, and in many languages.

It is out of these three decades plus of experience that I am sharing some observations, making some suggestions, and leaving you the reader to draw your own conclusions. This brief work has come to print at the request of some friends who are dealing with these issues at hand and asked for my comments.

These few pages are not meant to be exhaustive by any stretch of the imagination, and my thoughts and suggestions are simply meant to be just that. Obviously, every house of worship will have its own distinctives, strengths and weaknesses when it comes to the subject of corporate worship. What is thought to be right or appropriate will vary from place to place and will need to be determined ultimately by the Rabbi, Pastor or spiritual leader of the house.

I have observed many different traditions, likes and dislikes with regard to these different expressions, and have found some good guidelines that work for me. I will share some of these with you here and hope that you will find them useful and even helpful.

Paul Wilbur

ORDER IN THE COURTS!
AN INTROUCTION

I have once again finished re-reading the account of the dedication of Solomon's temple to the Lord in 2 Chronicles 5 through 7.
What an amazing spectacle that must have been! There were Le-
vitical priests preparing thousands of bulls, goats and lambs for
the sacrifices. Other Levites who were musicians appointed by
David stood in their places dressed in fine linen and playing cymbals, harps and lyres. Another 120 priests played trumpets while
large choirs of voices and many other instruments accompanied
them. Now how would you like to have been the one given the
responsibility to coordinate and direct that extravaganza? Cecil
B. DeMille would have been very proud of you! If only King David
could have lived to see that, he would have filled another whole
book of Psalms with a heart that could have exploded with the
site of it all!

It is obvious to me by this account (as well as many others) that all
these expressions of praise and worship are very pleasing to the
Lord. Not only the ministries described above, but also others including banners, flags, processionals, and dance were employed
to glorify the name of the Holy One of Israel. The question then is

not "if" we should utilize them, but rather "how" and "when."

I realize that in this new millennium many congregations and churches are using these instruments and expressions of worship in various ways and to different degrees. And so with this in mind, I will make some observations as to the "how" and "when" of some of these wonderful expressions of adoration and praise. My purpose and intention is clear; I want to so magnify the Lord that He is enthroned on our praises and manifests His power and presence so that all the earth will see His glory and join the procession!

CHAPTER 1

WHERE IT ALL BEGAN

"Can you help me with a problem?" was the way this pastor began our conversation. We had just finished a wonderful conference in his church in south Florida. "I'll try," I said with a hesitating voice. "I love all the expressions of worship," he continued, "the shofar, the banners and flags, the dancers, the tambourines...but I don't know what to do with them all! I really want to incorporate all the authentic elements of worship into our services, but it must be handled decently and in order. We just had such a wonderful time under your direction, so how do I implement these things in the worship of my church without looking like I'm quenching the Spirit, or leading a ministry where almost anything goes?"

I knew exactly what he meant. We want the pageantry and majesty without the flaky chaos that sometimes accompanies free expression. When should the shofar be used? Do we permit tambourines to be played? What about the banners and flags, prayer shawls, kippahs, and other garments of praise? What about the dancers? Do they really need so much space?

These are all great questions, and ones that will need to be answered sooner or later by the pastor, the elders, and the worship leader working in harmony with the vision of the house. As there are many different styles of leadership, as well as visions for corporate worship, I will simply share some guidelines that I believe work well, and leave the final decision for you to make.

EXTRAVAGANT WORSHIP AND JEWISH ROOTS

It seems to me that it was somewhere back in the 1970s when all these aforementioned questions became relevant. The songs of Jew's for Jesus like "Trees of the Field" and the groundbreaking ministry of Joel Chernoff and LAMB came crashing onto the fledgling contemporary Christian radio scene. These melodies and rhythms were different and fresh. No piano-organ duets with trombone solos that helped you take your afternoon siesta; these tunes made your foot tap along with the tambourine and dancing rhythms. The next thing you noticed was that most of the songs were written in minor keys and used the words of the prophets and the Psalms of David. A shofar, a few words in Hebrew and before you knew it you were standing on your feet and clapping your hands.

As this genre continued to expand with the music of David Loden, Israel's Hope and others, more questions began to arise. Is dancing a permissible form of worship in the sanctuary; can electric guitars and drum sets be used for worship; is this the time for the restoration of the tabernacle of David? Banners of the tribes of Israel are OK as decorations on the walls, but should they be processed and flown in the sanctuary?

Because this was more than just a musical style (in fact it was the beginnings of a Jewish revival), we had to deal with deeper issues that were at the root of the questions being asked. When Jews come to Messiah are they now Gentile Christians who should worship "the way we always have"? Is it right for them to worship on Shabbat and use some of those ancient liturgical prayers? What we really walked through early on was an Acts 15 council in reverse. This time the question was not, "How do we accept all these Gentiles into the faith of Israel's promised Messiah without requiring them to be fully converted Jews?" Rather, the questions were posed from a Gentile majority position of nineteen hundred years of practice and tradition!

As this modern messianic revival began we also had to deal with the articles of worship such as shofars, tambourines, minor keys, hand clapping, garments of praise expressed in Jewish worship (the tallis and yarmulke in particular), charismatic gifts, and additional forms of the arts. Whew, now that I think back on all this I wonder how we ever survived all the meetings, discussions, criticisms, and critics to become worshipers in spirit and in truth! The fact of the matter is that we were in the beginning of a full-blown revival of worship and the Word of God and didn't know it! But, didn't the apostle Paul state in Romans 11:15 that when Israel repented it would be "life from the dead"? And so, here we are some forty years later. In those early days it seemed like many of us pioneer messianic types were kicking against the goad of thousands of years of tradition without many listeners. But the times…they are a changin', as our Jewish musical prophet sang so many years ago.

With many churches singing the songs of Zion, building relationships with their Jewish neighbors, celebrating the Feasts of the Lord, and attending rallies in support of Israel this restoration of the tabernacle of David worship is really going to have an effect worldwide! This is a new day, I believe, and many of us will live to see the fruit of our earnest prayers and desires for the restoration of Israel and the church!

There is a role in this larger Broadway extravaganza for the modern Messianic Movement to play with regards to their calling and identity, but that large subject will have to wait for a future publication. They are called to be a voice in the wilderness for Israel, much like John the Baptist; an apostolic teacher in the church as the apostle Paul; a provoker in passionate biblical worship like King David; and at the same time to be a humble bridge of comfort and understanding between the nations and Israel. To that I would say... "Is that all, I'll get on that right away!"

THE CALL

It does strike me that the restoration of all these wonderful biblical expressions of praise and worship are a part of the calling and anointing on the modern messianic Jewish movement. The use of the instruments, the dance, the Hebrew; all of it seems to be right at home in the messianic services and celebrations. The feasts of the Lord, including the Sabbath (Lev. 23) along with the ancient words of the liturgy are all as comfortable here as that old blanket you used to cuddle up with at bedtime. This all makes sense in the Messianic Synagogue, but what about the Word of Faith churches, the Baptists and the Pentecostals? Simply stated, I am finding these expressions of worship in every country and in every denomination and language where I travel in the world. This is no longer an aberration among a few wild-eyed Jewish believers, this is a worldwide revival that will continue until the Messiah returns to take up His throne and receive all the worshipers in Jerusalem during the Feast of Tabernacles! (See Zechariah 14.)

Organizations such as Road to Jerusalem, Christians United for Israel, Toward Jerusalem Two, Bridges for Peace, the International Christian Embassy, and many others have all been birthed out of a growing revelation among the Gentile church. I believe that this seed will continue to grow and mature and influence the doctrine and the worship of the church (body of Messiah) all over the world. The Messianic Movement in Israel itself has multiplied many times over since my first trip there in 1983. More Jewish people have accepted Yeshua as Messiah in the last fifty years than in all the 1,900 years combined since the great Diaspora! These are exciting times of revelation as well as impartation and implementation, and we cannot burry our heads in the sand and hope that these people and their passion will somehow disappear. They are here to stay as a sign and an encouragement to look up because our Redeemer draws near and the restoration of all things is close at hand!

A QUICK LOOK BACK

This revival of worship that we are enjoying today is about forty years old by my calculation, and is entering into its second generation with maturity and grace. From the leadership and materials provided by Integrity, Maranatha, Vineyard, Hillsong, Zondervan, and others we are inheriting a rich history of modern praise and worship. It will be very important for our sons and daughters that we get these things right without some of the nonsense and religious bias we have already struggled through in the decades that preceded us.

Over the past forty years, we have wrestled with some of the biggest giants in this neighborhood and come out on top. Remember the silence of the service when the hymnals were removed from their places in the seat pocket in front of you? They were replaced with a spiral bound collection of "modern praise and worship choruses" that had all been written within the past two years! Some of them were directly extracted from the Scriptures, while others were simple love songs from the heart. Next thing we knew, these unwieldy songbooks were removed and we stood looking at large projection screens in front of the sanctuary where handwritten plastic sheets were projected with the lyrics so that our hands would be free to "praise the Lord." These were followed closely by typed versions, 35-millimeter slides, computer generated graphics, and now, full video presentations as savvy as the 10:00 o'clock news!

Next came the question as to which instruments are appropriate for the sanctuary. Acoustic guitars seemed to be fine, but what about those electric rock and roll versions with distortion, wa-wa pedals and all that go with them? Surely these cannot be permitted in our sanctuaries! Drums, percussion, and saxophones all came under similar scrutiny and had to be dealt with over time and with brave experimentation.

I will never forget a groundbreaking service that took place at Belmont Church in Nashville, Tennessee, in 1978. My group "Harvest" was invited to give a concert of praise one Sunday evening on a beautiful spring day in May. As we had arrived early in Nashville on Saturday evening, we decided to attend the AM service and see what one of America's premier Gospel Belt churches was up to. What we didn't know was that Belmont Church was a non-instrumental Church of Christ, which meant that musical instruments were not permitted to be used in sanctuary worship! What in the world were we doing here? Should we leave our instruments in their cases and sing everything acapella? Did we arrive at the right place but at the wrong time? This was, after all, the home church of Michael W. Smith, Brown Bannister and Amy Grant, along with many other notables of the growing Nashville gospel scene.

The service was going along just fine until Pastor Don Finto stood up and announced that they would be experiencing something new in praise and worship that morning. With that short introduction, Brown Bannister made his way to the platform and was joined by Amy Grant to lead some of those "modern choruses" with...their guitars! Well, you could have heard a pin drop in that large auditorium as the attention of the entire congregation was fixed on Brown and Amy. What we were witnessing firsthand was yet another breakthrough in the traditions of men that would liberate the people to worship God in spirit and in truth!

That evening the auditorium was packed to the rafters as the sounds of joy and praise filled the atmosphere. A revolution of worship and praise had begun in that city which has become the home for the creation and production of much of the contemporary Christian music we enjoy today. A bold move inspired by the Spirit would elevate the singing of praise songs from the place of preparation for the message to an expression of love and faith that would invite the manifest presence of God.

WITHOUT A VISION...

The beauty and majesty of all the artistic expressions belong in the sanctuary; I believe that with all my heart. Drama, music, dance, and artwork of all varieties can help us visually and emotionally as we seek to connect with God on every level of our lives. If we agree on that, then let's move forward with some thoughts on direction and vision for implementing this in our times of corporate worship.

This is a good place for me to make a couple of fundamental statements. First of all: "Ain't nothin' holy but the Lord!" The songs, the flags, the instruments, these are all great, but they are only elements to assist us in worship...they are *not* worship. Altars and incense were implemented to assist in worship; they were not what God was after, rather they helped in the giving of our hearts and devotion to the King. Tambourines, shofars, flags, and the garments of praise are not necessary for us to worship, but they are facilitators in our earthly expressions of our praise and worship. A popular song states, "It's all about You, Lord" and I believe this should be our guiding statement. When we get too caught up in all the "stuff" of who stands where, what are they wearing, or what they are playing, we have already missed the point of what we are there to do. Conversely, simply showing up in our jeans and t-shirts to "hang with the Dude upstairs" before running off to do some errands at the hardware and grocery store falls miserably short of the glorious life we have been called to live!

So with these thoughts in mind let's turn our attention to some of these elements that might interfere with our worship and put them in perspective. I believe that our purpose as pastors, worship leaders and worshipers is to make His praise glorious and His presence manifest both here "in Jerusalem, and in all Judea and Samaria, and to the ends of the earth" (Acts 1:8)!

CHAPTER 2

SHOFARS

Along with the renewed emphasis on praise and worship we are experiencing today, there has come a profound desire for the reality of His presence to accompany the experience. In other words, the people are no longer satisfied to simply sing the songs; they want to *experience* the presence of the God they worship! Perhaps Moses summed it up the best when he said to Adonai, "Now show me your glory" (Exod. 33:18). And because we are in a time of recapturing the roots of our faith, many new and exciting aspects of temple and tabernacle worship are being discovered and restored in our congregations and churches.

One of the instruments being restored to the sanctuary to-day is the shofar or ram's horn. Historically, this was an instrument sounded as a warning for battle, a call to assemble, and for worship. These instruments are also the ones mentioned in the Scriptures that are played by the angel of the Lord to wake the dead (1Thess. 4:16) and to gather the elect from the nations (Matt. 24:31).

The shortest shofars are made from the horn of a ram or male sheep and are approximately fifteen inches or so in length. They reflect back to the time when Abraham and Isaac were worshiping on the mountain, and God provided the ram caught in the thicket as a substitute for the life of Isaac. (See Genesis 22.) The shofar then becomes a constant reminder of God's faithfulness to fulfill the words He spoke through Abraham: "God himself will provide the lamb for the offering, my son." (Gen. 22:8) Every time we see or hear the shofar sounded it should remind us of the God of Abraham, Isaac and Jacob who keeps His covenant word to all generations!

The largest, and by far the loudest, of shofars are made from the horn of a large African animal called a Kudu. These large twisting horns are also known as Yemenite shofars and are quite capable of making a rather loud and invasive sound. When you hear the word *shofar* these are the instruments most people envision. They are majestic, ancient instruments that have the ability to stir the soul of man, and one day will signal the return of Messiah and wake the dead!

Other nations and cultures have adopted the shofar and made it their own using native materials that are available to them. I have seen elk antlers used in the Western parts of America and giant conch shells hollowed and cleaned for use in the Hawaiian Islands. All are appropriate, I believe, and are welcome to be played with skill and anointing in any of my services.

SOUND THE SHOFAR

Before going any further, let me first outline the areas for the use of the shofar traditionally, and then I will comment on its use in contemporary worship today.

In ancient times the shofar was played (or sounded) to:

Mark special times or seasons such as Rosh Hashanah (more correctly called Yom T'ruah, Day of Trumpets) the Feast of Tabernacles, etc. (Lev. 23)

1. **As a call to prayer and repentance.**
   (Lev. 23; Yom Kippur)

2. **A call to prepare for battle and to sound an alarm.**
   (1 Cor. 14:8)

3. **It was sounded at the receiving of the Torah on Sinai (Exod. 19)**

4. **It is a symbol of sacrifice (Abraham and Isaac, Gen. 22)**

5. **It will be heard from heaven to raise the dead (1 Thess. 4)**

6. **It will signal the return of Messiah (1 Thess. 4)**

7. **Worship (2 Chron. 5)**

First of all, please notice that I used the word *played* just before the list of times and purposes. I chose that word very carefully in order to make a point. That point is this; the shofar is a musical instrument that was to be played with skill and anointing. If we wouldn't ask a congregation to sit and listen to a rank beginner on a clarinet or violin, why do we ask them to put up with someone squawking on a shofar with no training, skill or anointing? Do we think perhaps that the people don't know the difference? Have you ever asked them? THEY DO! And it is somewhat pain-ful and embarrassing to be asked to sit quietly while someone struggles to get some kind of sound out of the instrument, not to mention make music or inspire us to worship! And if it is supposed to strike fear in the hearts of our enemies, I'm concerned that the only fear generated is in the hearts of the saints that their ears will be frequently attacked at our services!

SOME PRACTICAL ADVICE

If no one is in residence with the necessary skills, then I suggest that the shofar not be sounded at all. What about the frequently observed practice where everyone blows their shofar as often as they sense the anointing to do so? Well, should we invite all the guitar players to bring their instruments to service and play them whenever they feel inspired? Why not ask everyone who ever played a clarinet in junior high to bring their instrument with them to the service and just let it rip? Sounds ridiculous, I hope!

Since you trust your worship leader to lead the worship, perhaps you could trust him or her to give direction to the shofar playing as well. They could be responsible under the pastor's direction to give guidance and instruction for the playing of the shofar(s).

Here are some additional suggestions for the integration of the shofar into the worship of the congregation. The service could be started with the sounding of the shofar. If you are abundantly blessed with players, perhaps one could be sounded from all four corners of the sanctuary, calling the people to worship. Or, one player could sound the shofar to all four corners of the room. When the praise music warrants it, the shofar player could join the worship team in the playing of the instrument from the platform and into a microphone. It could be appropriate to allow everyone to sound their shofars at a heightened point of praise, say at the beginning of a song like "Let God Arise" or at the end of "Days of Elijah" when everyone is shouting and rejoicing. Those would be places for everyone with an instrument to "make a joyful noise unto the Lord" (Ps. 98:4, KJV). Otherwise, I would view the shofar as an instrument that is sounded as a part of the worship team and under the direction of the chief musician or worship leader.

I know this may cause some ruffling of the feathers at first, but it will bring order and peace to the congregation. Anyone who refuses to submit his or her instrument to the direction of spiritual leadership is a problem waiting to happen anyway, and so you might as well deal with it now. If someone enters the sanctuary with an instrument and is not a part of the worship team, an usher could gently direct them to the printed bulletin or the pre-service video for direction with regards to their instrument. An announcement could be made prior to the beginning of each service simply stating the policy of the house regarding instruments played in the congregation. If you print a weekly bulletin, the "rules of the house" could be announced there or depicted with grace and a little humor during a pre-service video presentation.

What do I do if I want to have the sound of the instrument but I don't have a trained and anointed player? Do what I do when my shofar player is not out with me on the road. I had my keyboard player "sample" the sound of the shofar into the memory banks of his instrument. Any time I need that sound it is available with the nod of my head. In this form, the shofar is always in tune with any song we play, and is also perfectly played every time!

SPONTANAITY

Fine, but what about the place for spontaneous celebration and praise? Is there no more room for expressions that are not dictated from the platform? Of course there is! In fact, let me say this to some of you who are wondering where this is all headed. I would rather bring some order and correction to a passionate house of praisers than to lead worship in a valley of dry bones! I would definitely prefer to ask everyone to take a deep breath than to constantly be checking to see if anyone out there has a pulse! I love the passion and zeal of some of you "charismaniacs" for the Lord and His house. You are the ones who make my job a real joy. (Can you feel the love I am sending your way?)

Now to those of you who have never danced in the aisle, waved a banner, shouted with all your heart, or tried to make a shofar sound like a musical instrument. If you have been enjoying these words spoken to all those "worship nuts," let me give you a gentle word or two as well. I won't try to convince you here of the incredible blessing and personal benefits to be experienced for being a passionate, expressive worshiper. I will simply say be careful not to become judgmental about your brothers and sisters when they worship. Remember, they are not worshiping or praising you, but rather, they are worshiping the Lord of Glory.

JUDGE NOT...

In 1 Chronicles 15:29, King David's wife Michal despised her husband's worship as he led the procession to bring the Ark of the Covenant up to Jerusalem. She judged his heart and motives, and she completely dismissed the fact that her husband was so in love with Jehovah that he could have cared less about what he was or was not wearing. He wasn't showing off his buff physique for the young women of Jerusalem, he was desperate for the pleasure of his God! Her judgmental attitude so angered the Lord that her womb was shut up and she could not bear any children. I believe the spiritual significance of all this is more than obvious. Jesus said:

> *Do not judge, or you too will be judged. For in the same way you judge others, you will be judged, and with the measure you use, it will be measured to you. ... You hypocrite, first take the plank out of your own eye, and then you will see clearly to remove the speck from your brother's eye.* (*Matt. 7:1,2,5*)

We have not been given a spirit of judgment but of discernment. Discernment is a spiritual gift that will give us the understanding we need to deal with a person or situation in a godly way to bring resolve and restoration. Judgment will be polarizing, and it brings out opinionated arguments causing sides to form. I have heard it said that "opinions are like noses, everyone has one!" Our personal opinions are not important here, but rather, what does the Lord think about all this. I have learned over the years to hold my thoughts for a while until I can see what kind of fruit the tree is bearing. It is only then that you can know if the tree is good or bad. James says it like this: "Everyone should be quick to listen, slow to speak and slow to become angry" (James 1:19). Be patient with things you don't understand; your opinion could change tomorrow!

FINDING OUR WAY

I am suggesting that each house of worship must teach and demonstrate what good, acceptable practice is for that congregation. This can be done in a gracious and loving way that does not "quench the Spirit" and gives freedom as well as order to the corporate expressions. What is demonstrated from the platform is the strongest way to teach a congregation what is good and acceptable in that sanctuary.

The worship leader working in harmony with a loving and caring team of ushers can move the vision of the house forward without offending visitors or smothering a breakout of the high praises of God when joy overtakes the celebration. Again, the vision set forth by the leadership, taught by the pastor and demonstrated by the worship team will be the blueprint for the house.

Here is another resource for you to consider. Two of the biggest problems with purchasing a shofar for use in the sanctuary are pitch (the actual notes the instrument is capable of sounding) and "playability" (how easily the horn can be sounded). My friend Randy Spencer in Houston, Texas is not only a master player of the shofar, but he also builds and tunes his horns for both pitch and playability. If you desire to speak with him about an instrument, he can be reached through his Web site at www.trumpetsofgod.com. These handcrafted instruments will help make a master player out of your aspiring priesthood no matter what their level of experience might be!

CHAPTER 3

TAMBOURINES

"So listen while I play...my green tambourine." That's how the lyric went to a very annoying song of the 60s. Why was the song so bothersome? What's wrong with green tambourines? Truthfully, green tambourines are not the problem; neither are red ones or even those made in the shape of a Star of David with bright colorful streamers! They are very exciting percussion instruments when placed in the hands of *skilled* musicians. The problem with *your* tambourine is this: if you are going to play it, we all have to listen!

Yes, I used the words *play* and *skill* again on purpose. The tambourine is an ancient instrument found in Greece, Rome and the Middle East. It is a member of the *percussion* family of instruments, which are defined as "the group of instruments that produce sound by being struck, including drums and cymbals." The modern tambourine harkens back to a Middle Persian instrument called a *tambur*, which means "lute, drum." It is also referred to as a *tabret* in the Scriptures and is used in many different ways. The tambourine is basically a hand drum that comes in many sizes and shapes, but was traditionally round with an animal skin stretched over one side. Early on, there were just a few jangles added to the rim for additional sound. These "jangles" are small round pieces of metal that look like miniature cymbals and are placed opposite each other so they strike together when the instrument is shaken or struck. As of late, some modern tambourines have many more jangles and no skin whatsoever, but remain *very* loud, commanding percussion instruments.

There is an Arabic version of the tambourine called a "tambour" that an Arab believer introduced me to during the recording of "Shalom Jerusalem" way back in 1995. When I first saw the tambour I thought to myself, "this thing is too small to be heard over the orchestra, choir and band in this large hall." Man, was I wrong! When the young man gave me a brief demonstration of his instrument's capabilities, I was blown away. That little thing sounded like a complete drum set and could be heard throughout the entire auditorium of 3,500 seats with no problem

SOME CHALLENGES

When we speak about the tambourine we are dealing with yet another musical instrument intended to be played with skill and anointing. One problem we run into as leaders is that some people use these instruments for their own private worship at home and then bring them to the sanctuary so they can continue their worship experience there. They are not trained musicians, yet they are passionate and sincere worshipers, dedicated intercessors, and wholehearted praisers of the Lord who we do not want to discourage or offend. Part of my motivation in writing these words is to help some folks see the problems leaders face with the public, unordered use of these instruments in the sanctuary, so there will be grace and understanding. I believe the next couple of paragraphs will help clear up some of these misunderstandings and bring a sense of clarity to my reasoning here.

THE CALL TO UNITY

My good friend Don Potter offered the following thoughts on "the call to unity" to me some years ago, and I believe it to be some great material to share with you here. Although I have completely embraced what he spoke to me and have made it my own, I need to give him credit for the content.

Why did Miriam choose a tambourine to celebrate the Lord's great victory on the other side of the sea? One reason is that it would be heard over thousands of voices outside with no microphones or sound systems! Selah. Another reason for her choice of this instrument is that the tambourine is an instrument with the ability to sound a *call to unity*. What do I mean by that? The percussion instruments are a bold call to unity because they demand that all other instruments and voices submit to their leadership! I may be a worship leader who leads the worship team, but my drummer is the one who is calling the entire band to unity behind him as he sets the tempo and the feel for the song. If he decides to follow a different course there is nothing I can do with my guitar and voice to gain the upper hand. In other words, percussion instruments sound a clear direction that all other instruments will follow.

I am blessed to work with some of the very best drummers in Christian music today who travel with me as a part of our worship team. Several years ago during a worship conference we hosted in Nicaragua, I listened in on a class as my drummer was instructing his group of percussionists. He was stressing the importance of playing as a unified team rather than a group of individuals. Then he made a statement to his class that I will never forget. He was comparing the different instruments in a worship band to the mechanical parts of a bus. He said the bass player was the under frame that the entire bus rested on; I liked that. The worship leader was the gas pedal and brake that controlled the ebb and flow; I liked that too. Then he said… "But I drive the bus!" Now, all the drummers signaled their immediate approval with loud laughter and applause. "What?" I thought, "He drives my bus?" Yes, and there is nothing I can do about it if he decides to turn left when I want to go right!

Although drummers are the brunt of many a cruel musical joke*, make no doubt about it, they are a very important part of the team. Drums and percussion definitely do drive the bus and command the attention of all those under the sound of their instruments. That is simply the way it is. Bigger is not necessarily better, but louder is always king!

Now if I (and my percussionists) are calling for unity from the platform, and Sister Pentecost is calling for unity with her tambourine from row seven, and Brother Bo Jangles is calling for unity with his tambourine from the balcony...what do we have? That's right; chaos and confusion, and God is certainly not the author of any of that! (See 1 Corinthians 14:33.)

*How do you get a drummer to play softer? Put music in front of him!

MUTINY OR SCIENCE?

The challenges we face with these instruments in the sanctuary are not necessarily rebellious or prideful spirits (although that could be a potential problem with some individuals), but a large part of the problem we face is simply the science of acoustics. Because of time delay and reflecting surfaces, it is impossible for even skilled musicians to play together when scattered around an auditorium. Now if we take the "skilled" part out of the equation as well, we are left with an overwhelming and insurmountable problem!

Does this sound like I'm exaggerating in order to make a point? I assure you that I most certainly am not! In one church in Pittsburgh, there were so many tambourines in the sanctuary that the pastor stopped the service in order to receive an offering... a tambourine offering! Thank God for him! He happens to be a very musical pastor who understands and appreciates good music as well as orderly worship. You would not believe the number of instruments surrendered in that *first* tambourine offering in Pittsburgh. I said "first" because he received a *second* offering when all the instruments were not handed over the first time!

The tambourine is designed to be loud. It is designed to lead. You have to make the decision as to *who* will lead the praise and worship in your congregation. Have you ever had the distinct pleasure of standing beside someone "playing" his or her tambourine during worship? It is distractive at best, and more like completely overpowering at the worst. Again, I am not trying to be critical or cute. These are very real challenges that must be met with prayerful consideration and sensitive leadership.

A LITTLE HELP FROM MY FRIENDS

So, what do we do? I have a suggestion or two. If you want tambourines played in the sanctuary, have them join the worship team, practice with the musicians, and submit to the leadership of the chief musician or worship leader. I would announce before each service that personal tambourines are to be placed under your chair and played only when directed by the worship leader. They are great for your personal times of praise and

worship at home, but they are not to be played at your discretion during corporate times of worship in the sanctuary. I have also found that teaching on the spiritual aspect of *the call to unity* is helpful for people to hear the reasoning behind the decision and keep them from being unnecessarily offended or embarrassed.

Some want freedom without limitations while others want limitations without freedom. We will see later that the apostle Paul taught the Corinthians what is best for all: freedom within the boundaries.

TAKING CONTROL

I was in a conference of worship several years ago, when a man holding *four* tambourines moved into the center isle and shook his instruments continually, regardless of the tempo or feel of the music. Now some may have felt that he was being moved by the Spirit of God and that somewhere in this mess there was a hidden message for us. Who was I to judge his worship? Maybe he was a prophet sent to enlighten us all! It wasn't long before the people stopped praising God and began to focus upon this man and what his actions could mean. So...before too many more seconds went by I called two ushers to the platform and asked them to have the man surrender his tambourines and his newly assumed role as worship leader. A brief moment of tension ensued when the gentleman hesitated to give up his instruments and return to his seat. Thankfully, he did so without a need for further intercession or correction! It was very interesting to me that as soon as the incident passed, praises intensified again with a renewed joy and peace. The people knew this was a safe environment where order prevailed and they were once again able to focus their affection and attention on the Lord and His majesty instead of the man with his four tambourines.

So was I being a control freak? Was I suffocating the individual expression of that dear man and his worship of God? The answer I believe is a resounding "NO!" I was liberating the house from an occupying force. Any modestly mature man or woman will gladly submit to the godly authority of the house they are worshiping in without a hassle; all others need to be corrected and encouraged by mature leadership.

ALTERNATIVES?

Here are some more thoughts for you to consider as the worship leader or pastor of the congregation. You might want to allow tambourines, but only the ones that have no jangles on them. I have seen some people take a tambourine frame and fix short (ten inches or less) colored streamers to the rim in order to fashion a silent instrument of praise. It works! (More on this in the chapter, *Silence is Golden*) They get to participate in the praise without competing with the praise and worship team for the call to unity.

You may also want to permit corporate tambourine playing along with the corporate shofar sounding during special times of high praises that I described earlier. You may organize a team of tambourine players that minister during special music. Other than these examples, I would not allow the free playing of tambourines or shofars during corporate worship.

At first, some people will think you are not very spiritual by taking away their personal musical offerings to the Lord. But I promise you that the rest of the congregation will be very grateful for the direction; and the folks who came to worship the Lord will be free to do so without needless distractions and challenges. Again, any time individuals become the focus of attention during corporate worship they are out of order and a problem that will need to be addressed.

WHERE THE SPIRIT OF THE LORD IS...

You may be asking, "So where does the spirit of liberty end and chaos begin?" It is very interesting to me as I travel around the world to observe the many different styles of worship and the rules by which they are governed. Some love every expression all the time. Others permit some expressions during certain times and in specific places, while others aren't having any of the extravagant expressions ever! I believe we must keep in mind that when we come together as a body that the individual freedoms and expressions we enjoy privately must submit to the goal of serving the greater body of Messiah. In other words, if my private practice of worshiping the Lord "as David did" by dancing wildly around my apartment in my Fruit of the Looms is not edifying to the whole church, then I must lay that expression down when we all come together. Amen!

Just as the father sets the rules and example in each household, so the pastor must set the boundaries in each house of worship.

Some will say, "But I can't live with these rules." Then I suggest that you find a house where you can. However, if you have been to seven congregations in the past two months and none of them understand your highly prophetic call to play your tambourine, shofar and harp whenever you sense that ministering angels are on assignment, maybe it's time to re-examine your ministry!

CHAPTER 4

FLAGS AND BANNERS

The use of banners and flags has a long and important history in the lives of nations, armies and celebrations. The banners and the flags can be beautiful expressions of faith that will stir our hearts and emotions to praise and adoration. In Psalm 20:5, King David declares, "We ... will lift up our banners [or flags] in the name of our God." Banners and flags are also used as a sign of purpose or intent. In Psalm 74:4 the enemies of the Lord "set up their standards as signs." Signs of what? Signs of their intentions to destroy the people of God who were gathered there! Flags of the nations usually tell us something about the nation they represent. Banners are carried at the front of an army in order to distinguish the men from other armies or divisions. They alert the observer as to the capabilities, rankings, training, and expertise of those under their colors.

Have you ever seen the national flags raised at the medal ceremonies during the Olympic games? Why do so many of the athletes cry during those brief moments when their nations are exalted because of their own personal achievements? The reason is the flags and banners accompanied by the national anthems are very strong reminders of who they are and the people they represent. They make a very strong emotional connection to a land, a people and a destiny. Flags and banners can stir a very powerful sense of ethnic or national pride.

The Lord Himself raises a banner over His own people. In fact, one of His covenant names is *Jehovah Nissi*, the Lord our Banner! In Song of Solomon 2:4 we read, "His *banner* over [us] is love" (emphasis added); in Psalm 60:4 He gives His people a *banner* of truth to be unfurled by those who fear Him. In Psalm 20:5 we read, "We will shout for joy when you are victorious, and will lift up our *banners* in the name of our God" (emphasis added). Banners set boundaries, make declarations, state a purpose, and ignite emotions. They can be very powerful expressions in praise and worship when properly used under an anointing. Remember that *anointing* is not some spooky spiritual word with no real definition, rather it is the power or ability to accomplish a Spirit-inspired task. If we agree that there is an anointing to preach (IS.61:1), and to sing, and to play an instrument, and to teach the Word of God, then I would also say that there is an anointing to minister before the Lord and His people with flags and banners!

Another story, if I may. It was during the taping of "Shalom Jerusalem" in Israel in March of 1995. The last song to be sung that evening was a very stirring anthem entitled, "Lord, Take Up Your Holy Throne." Everything was going great. The recording was filled with moments we would all remember for a lifetime and we were winding down to the final big anthem. As we sang, "Lord, take up your holy throne, throughout all the earth" a HUGE banner was processed to the front with the message and image of THE LION OF JUDAH. The people cheered and stood to their feet; the music swelled...and our lead trumpet player was so overwhelmed by it all that he couldn't play the final big fanfare! He was reduced to tears as the emotion of the reality of the scenario flooded his heart and soul. The sites and sounds work together to bring us a fuller revelation of a spiritual reality of heavenly things. The horn part was fixed later in the studio, but the moment of awe and majesty is fixed forever in our hearts and imaginations. I love it!

A DOUBLE-EDGED SWORD

Having just said all that, there is another side to this coin. Yes, the banners are beautiful, powerful statements in worship, but they can also be weapons of warfare that are capable of maiming the poor unfortunates on the aisles and front rows! Flagpoles and whipping fabrics can have a devastating effect when they come in sudden contact with an unsuspecting worshiper. It is not uncommon today to have an established ministry for the flags and banners who meet for instruction and direction and rehearsal with regards to the proper use of the flags in a house of worship. Each congregation will have different guidelines for their use, and it would be a good idea to express that both publicly and in a training session with those who wish to participate. The large banners and flags require a great deal of strength and skill to handle properly and are dangerous to trust into the hands of the novice and the uninitiated.

Like the music and musicians, I believe the banners are special elements of praise and worship that need some understanding and training in order to use them effectively in the corporate setting. As the head goes, so goes the rest of the body or ministry. Be thoughtful and discerning as to the ones you place over this ministry. I personally have a problem with miscellaneous flag waving in the congregation for several reasons. One reason is that they are dangerous! Sticks and poles in the hands of children and some enthusiastic adults make me nervous. The other reason is that it is disorganized and distractive to people sitting or standing near those who are participating.

Where do I find the right person for this ministry? Just as in the other areas of responsibility, the ones who are making and using the flags are probably the ones to direct their use. Kenaniah was chosen by King David to lead the choir as the Ark was being brought up to Jerusalem "because he was skillful at it" (1 Chron. 15:22). There are many conferences on praise and worship where people can get some great training and ideas for the banner ministry of your church. A submitted person who works well with others and has a healthy respect for the presence of the Lord will be a good leader for the banners and flags. They should be used in conjunction with the worship leader and placed under the direction of the worship ministry. Although I agree that in general they should not become a focus or distraction, there may be times when the flags actually *become* the message that the Lord is bringing forth. Banners that are well made and skillfully displayed can be a powerful encouragement to the entire house to worship.

TABERNACLE WITH US

When you think of banners and flags, you are probably remembering a typical experience where the larger banners are processed and the smallish flags are waved in a static way. Here are a few experiences I have had with exceptional ministries under a wonderful anointing with incredible results.

I remember a conference in Columbus, Ohio where I was ministering with my "Holy Fire" CD back in the late 90s. As I began to sing the opening lines of the title track, a tall man in white garments came running in carrying a very tall pole with a fifteen-foot flag on top that looked like it was on fire! He ran to the front of the sanctuary and began to wave the flaming flag back and forth. The people shouted, the praises soared to the heavens, and the atmosphere was electrified! I can still close my eyes and see the scene played out in living color after all these years; fabulous!

There is a tremendous ministry out of Blacksburg, Virginia called Messiah Dance Company (www.messiahcompany.org). They have traveled and ministered with us all over the world. During one service of intimate worship, they brought out long banners that were deep red in color, took hold of each end, and slowly floated them just above the heads of the people signifying the covering of the blood of the Lamb. The worshipers began to reach up to touch the banners as they glided overhead. What a beautiful and moving scene that was. A simple point of contact with a powerful message for us all!

On another occasion in Ghana, West Africa, our dance team brought two large silks about thirty feet long that were beautifully hand painted with biblical scenes on each of the four corners. During the song "In Your Presence," they formed a moving silk tabernacle in the front of the room. The people began to come from all over the sanctuary to sit and sing underneath the silks until I believe the entire crowd of several thousand had an opportunity to experience this special place. Reports of healing, comfort and deliverance abounded in that service because of the sensitive ministry of the dance and banner team; praise the Lord!

CHAPTER 5

PRAISE HIM WITH THE DANCE!

Over the years, I have heard many different comments from people about the ministry of dance. This is one arena where the opinions are strong and rather polarizing. When, where, how, and even *if* dance is appropriate, which kind, how many, how often, what should or should not be worn; all this and more are up for discussion when it comes to this subject. So, in my opinion, the only opinion worth hearing is the Lord's opinion! In Psalm 149:2-3, King David declares, "Let Israel rejoice in their Maker; let the people of Zion be glad in their King. Let them praise his name with dancing…"

I was personally introduced to the joy and power of dance back in the early 1980s through the life and ministry of Mikhael Murnane and Jerusalem Worship Dance Company. Later I met Son Dance, Randall Bane, Todd Farley, and many others too numerous to name here. Over the past few years, we have partnered with many of these pioneers to celebrate the Lord through praise and worship. Our friends Barry and Lana Portnoy now accompany us to demonstrate the power and anointing in celebrating the Feasts of the Lord in Leviticus chapter 23; Messiah Dance Company has traveled with us to Africa and Central America, and we meet more new and exciting ministers of dance all over the world!

I personally love the ministry of dance in all of its forms. It is an expression of joy in worship and praise that can ignite the people to a place of freedom and deliverance. You may think I'm over-exaggerating my point here, but I simply don't believe that I am. I have watched for many years as the dance ministry has set the house on fire with a passion to exalt the Lord. Movement gives the human body an opportunity to be a living sacrifice and an expression of beauty and humility in worship. I have also seen dance used as an offering of faith that brought freedom from sickness and spiritual bondage.

Dance can be an exuberant celebration of praise for a great victory or simply a humble movement to express the joy of intimacy. I love the story of the prodigal son in Luke 15. The father's heart was so full of praise and thanksgiving at his son's return that his whole house was filled with the sound of music *and* dancing. In Ecclesiastes 3:4, the author reminds us that there is "a time to mourn and a time to dance." And who could ever forget the vision of King David dancing before the Lord and the Ark of the Covenant with ALL his might in 1 Chronicles 15:29? Most certainly there is a time and place for dance in the house of the Lord!

We have all had many different experiences with dance I'm sure, both good and bad. But as a worship leader I would rather have to reign in a thoroughbred than be relegated to beating a dead horse. In other words, give me a congregation of passionate people who need instruction, but don't make me the overseer of a funeral home!

ALL TOGETHER NOW

Without gifted and anointed leadership and direction, the ministry of dance can digress into something no one really wants to see. As always, the success or failure of any group activity will rest with the quality and direction of the leadership. I believe that public ministry brings with it a responsibility of skill with excellence both in the discipline itself as well as in spirit. Everyone will recognize the difference between a song leader who waves his hand at the congregation during the three hymns and a worship leader. The results speak for themselves. In the same manner, anyone can tell the difference between someone who *likes* to dance and someone who is *anointed* to dance.

Dancers, like musicians can be very independent and opinionated, but when the right attitude is matched with anointing the results can be spectacular. There are several ways for the dance to be included in your praise and worship. Some songs may be "choreographed" with specific dancers, garments and movements. Processionals with banners and flags to begin a service are majestic and capture the congregation's attention right from the start. These same dancers can invite and orchestrate times of free dance expressions with the congregation and give direction and order to that time.

Some congregations offer dance instruction for those who wish to add some training to their feet. This is great for fellowship as well as worship team growth, and gives the leaders an excellent opportunity to identify others who may be called to the dance ministry of your congregation. The dance can be used as presentational, corporate or individual worship for specials during the offering or to express a truth to introduce or enhance a message. It could be performed by an individual with exceptional training and anointing or presented by a team who are well rehearsed.

The dance ministry can be limited to a specific space in the sanctuary. Instruction and direction needs to be given from the pulpit and enforced with kindness and understanding from the floor by the ushers and dance leaders. Yes, it takes time, energy, forethought, and vision to have a successful and anointed time of dance and extravagant worship, but I believe the results far outweigh the effort.

Now I am not a historian, nor am I someone schooled in the social sciences; however, I am willing to wager that there has never been a culture of any size in the history of mankind that didn't have dancing associated with it. From the bouncing and twirling of the African tribes to the measured discipline of the ballet, dance is a part of our lives; why not in the kingdom of God? All in favor...

LIKE HINDS FEET

I was invited to share a platform several years ago with a dance troupe made up of hundreds of children. *Uh oh,* you might be thinking, *here's an opportunity for disaster.* I would agree with you if it weren't for the mature guidance and leadership provided by Ann Stevenson, the head of that ministry. The children were incredible! Their hands, feet and lips were disciplined into an expression of praise that brought the congregation to their feet time and time again shouting for more. Some of the songs were sung two or three times in succession because of the reaction of the congregation!

In another worship conference there were many dancers and dance ministries in attendance who were familiar with my music and were anxious to participate in the service in some way. Again, you might think that this would be THE recipe for disaster, chaos and confusion. But, thanks to the many mature and anointed leaders who were there, the whole service turned out to be a corporate worship of song and dance that no one wanted to end! After the service, I went to the "green room" for some refreshments with the other guests. There was an international minister there from Scotland who I had wanted to meet for some time. He sat at the table with me and began to speak very slowly as if the words were difficult to form in his mind. "Paul," he said, "I have never been in a service like that... I am completely blown away. You need to capture this on video as instruction and a blessing to all who will see it. I know what I am talking about; you need to do this."

Well, needless to say, I was blessed and encouraged by his words. But how do you restage something that the Holy Spirit produced without any human direction or intention? Again, the success of the evening was largely due to the worship dance instructors who were in the middle of the congregation giving direction and order to what could have been a complete fiasco.

While I was in Hawaii on the island of Maui I observed yet another approach to dance ministry. The dancers in this contemporary church were made up of teens and young adults. They never left the stage, but were carefully placed among the musicians up on the platform. I have never seen a dance ministry used this way, but I thought it was effective and inspiring. I would probably use this model if I were leading worship for the youth or young adults; it was very cool!

There are many opportunities to grow and mature a dance ministry today with all the conferences and seminars available. Videos and books by some of the most prominent instructors are easily obtained if you know where to look for them. The Internet is a good place to start as many of the best dance ministries today have a Web site where you can learn and purchase materials. (Just be very careful that when you Google for dancers online that you add the word "ministry"!) The dance is a ministry of joy and freedom when under the leadership of anointed people. So whether the ministry is limited to those who have trained and practiced or it is extended to the entire congregation, let the people praise Him with the dance!

CHAPTER 6

THE PROPHETIC VOICE

Over the past few years, we have been enjoying a revival of the prophetic ministry. Amazingly accurate voices like Bob Jones, Kim Clement and Chuck Pierce have brought an excitement and trust back into this vital and timely ministry revival. This has followed a revival of the Word of God and worship that has spanned the last four decades. By the way, these great moves of the Spirit of God have been paralleled by a quiet and timely revival amongst the Jewish community worldwide. More Jews have come to the saving knowledge of Yeshua in the past forty years than in all 1900 years combined since the Diaspora! Just a coincidence...I hardly think so! There are some wonderful resources that document this prophetic event much better than I could do here. Paul Lieberman's book *A Fig Tree Blossoms* is a good place to start (it is available on our Web site at www.wilburministries.com).

There is a divine ordering of all this that makes perfect sense to me, and here's why. Over the last forty years or so (a biblical generation) we have heard from pastors and teachers about the preeminence of the Word of God. Bible teachers like Kenneth

Hagin, Joyce Meyer, Kenneth Copeland and Dr. Charles Stanley have taught us to read, believe, meditate on, and confess the Scriptures on a daily basis. At the same time, we have also been in a forty-year revival of praise and worship. Names like Chuck Girard, Keith Green, Bill Gaither and many others come to mind as I remember the early days of scripture choruses, Full Gospel Business Men's Fellowship meetings and women's Aglow. So, with the forty-year foundation of the Word and worship, the Lord is now laying the prophetic ministry over the top. We need to hear what the Spirit is saying to us today, right now, if we are going to be fully equipped for the task at hand. Again, the instructions will be tailor-made to fit the people, the house, the city, and the nation. This is definitely NOT a "one size fits all" kind of ministry. Therefore, we need to plan for and make room for the voice of the Lord in our corporate times of worship and praise.

WORSHIP AND THE PROPHETIC

Follow the way of love and eagerly desire spiritual gifts, especially the gift of prophecy. ...But everyone who prophesies speaks to men for their strengthening, encouragement and comfort. ...but he who prophesies edifies the congregation.
(1 Corinthians 14:1,3,4 NIV)

Calling to and listening for the prophetic voice is one of the primary functions of corporate praise and worship. True worship puts our hearts and minds in a position and attitude to receive the voice of the Holy Spirit in our midst! Remember when the prophet Elisha was called to prophesy before King Joram and King Jehoshophat in 2 Kings 3:15? He had only one request...*send me a minstrel* (musician or harpist). A musician or minstrel operating in the anointing can be a sledgehammer to break through the natural and usher us into the prophetic realm. God surely does inhabit the praises of His people (Ps. 22:3, KJV) and in His presence there is fullness of joy with pleasures at His right hand forevermore (Ps. 16:11). There is a holy marriage between worship and the prophetic that cannot be denied, and certainly should not be ignored.

So, however you decide to handle it, we need to make provision and preparation for the gifts of the Holy Spirit once again. In fact, my understanding of true worship in a nutshell is this: we bow to honor but also to hear (shachah), and we stand to obey the God who sees (Yireh). In Genesis chapter 22, Abraham said to his servants, "Stay here … while I and the boy go over there. We will worship [shachah] and then we will come back to you" (v. 5). This was obviously an immense statement of faith on Abraham's part, as he knew what the Lord had told him to do on the mountain. As Abraham raised the knife to obey the word of God, the angel of the Lord (Malach Adonai) told him to put his knife down because NOW He knew Abraham truly feared or worshiped (Yireh) the Lord. To worship is to bow in adoration and submission to hear and then to stand up and to obey the Lord who speaks and sees all. These are the kind of worshipers that Yeshua told the Samaritan woman about in John 4. These are the kind of worshipers the Father is still seeking today!

WHAT ARE WE REALLY DOING HERE?

Please remember that one of the greatest effects our praise and worship accomplishes as we send it forth is this…WE ARE TAKING CONTROL OF THE ATMOSPHERE! This is a tactic used by any modern army when they are moving into enemy territory. First, the commander will send in the air force in order to take control of the air space above the battlefield and to destroy the major defensive and communication devices of the enemy. Once this is accomplished, the army moves in on the ground without fear that they will be taken out by enemy forces overhead. Next, major landscape is secured, command centers are established, and what was once hostile territory becomes a base of operations. Remember what Yeshua said, "…the kingdom of heaven has been forcefully advancing, and forceful men lay hold of it" (Matt. 11:12). Another translation puts it this way: "… the kingdom of heaven suffers violence, and the violent take it by force" (NKJV).

The Lord Himself is seated or enthroned upon the praises of His people (Ps. 22:3, NKJV). When God arises, He will scatter His enemies. In 1 Corinthians 14:8 the apostle Paul states, "For if the trumpet makes an uncertain sound, who will prepare himself for battle?" (NKJV). It is important then, that when we pray or praise that something is actually accomplished in the Spirit. Praise and worship is not merely some musical, spiritual exercise that prepares us to receive the morning message; no, true worship is strategic and essential, and is an end, in and of itself! This is one reason the Scriptures say to "send Judah first." Every time we gather for worship, someone or something will take control of the atmosphere. Will it be chaos and confusion or the divine order of the presence of the Holy One of Israel? We make the choice!

Why did Jehoshaphat send the worship team out into the valley ahead of the army? (This is a great example of the prophetic voice working in harmony with the worship team to exact a tremendous blow against the enemy!) In 2 Chronicles 20, the kings of Moab and of Ammon along with some Meunites marched together against Judah to destroy the now divided kingdom of the Jews.

When the report of the advancing armies reached Jehoshaphat ,he called for a national day of prayer in order to hear what the Lord had to say about all this. As they worshiped and prayed a Levite descendant of Asaph, named Jahaziel, stepped forward to speak the word of the Lord. Let me condense his message for the sake of space. Basically the prophet said, "Do not be afraid; the battle is not yours but the Lord's. March out against them and do not be afraid. Stand firm and see the deliverance of the Lord. Do not be afraid for the Lord will be with you!" (For Jahaziel's actual speech, see 2 Chronicles 20:14–17.)

Did you notice the recurring theme of faith? The message of "do not be afraid" is really hard to miss. The point to me here is that the manifest presence of God produces confidence and faith. If we want our congregations to be full of faith and confidence in the Lord, then we need to be places where His presence and voice are manifest on a regular basis! So, armed with the Word of Jehovah, Jehoshaphat sent the singers out ahead of the army singing, "Give thanks to the Lord, for his love endures forever" (v. 21). As they began to sing and praise, the God who 'inhabits the praises of His people' showed up and kicked some enemy *tuchas!* (Just a little Yiddish term for the hind parts of the anatomy.)

We need to understand that when we come together in corporate praise and worship we are entering a tactical battle zone. We are on assignment just as the forces that oppose us are on assignment from their commander-in-chief. The worship, the prayers and the praises of the righteous are powerful and effective and they will prevail. The weapons of our warfare are not carnal, or natural, but they are mighty through God for the pulling down of those strongholds (2 Cor. 10:4, NKJV)!

PREPARING FOR HIS PRESENCE

Yes, it does take time, energy and prayerful preparation to prepare a place for the manifest presence of God. We could however, escape all this planning and preparation if all we want is a well ordered service. We can have that in 55 minutes flat; complete with song service (15 minutes), announcements (5 minutes), video presentation of coming events (5 minutes), baby dedication (5 minutes), and a message (25 minutes). But I would suggest to you that if our corporate times of *worship* are consistently relegated to this kind of format, we are definitely cheating ourselves as well as our people from the most fulfilling moments of life… the manifest presence of God in the midst of His people!

I have traveled the world and ministered with Pastor Benny Hinn in some of the largest stadiums and churches of the world. It is always of great interest to me to note how much time is spent in those crusades preparing a place for the presence and power of the Holy Spirit. It appears to me that many of the greatest miracles take place during the extended time of worship. Yes, there are prayer teams in the crowds who anoint the sick with oil and pray the prayer of faith, but there is something about the manifest presence of God in worship that brings faith to bear and seals the deal. By the time these worshipers come to the stage to testify, the ministry and presence of the Holy Spirit has already healed them! Now you may not agree with everything that happens or with everything that is said in every meeting, but I have never met a man who honors and respects the presence and ministry of the Holy Spirit like Benny Hinn. (When people ask my opinion about the famous people I travel and minister with, I tell them that if I listened to myself long enough I would hear things I didn't agree with as well!)

I know we all wrestle with timeliness and busy lives. Some pastors have to get thousands of people in and out on a Sunday morning with a tight time schedule because of the size of the auditorium; I understand that, but what about Sunday night, Wednesday night, or a Friday night service that is dedicated to worship and prayer as well as the Sabbath? When we are finished, we are finished. No time limits and no other people to get in and out. Yes, I would have an agenda and a schedule, but with plenty of grace for the moment when the Lord really begins to move, with the understanding that HIS voice and ministry is the whole reason we get together! Like the song says, "It's all about you, Lord!"

This is one of the aspects that I would call the "fathering" heart of the pastor. As it is with raising children in a home, it takes time, patience, and all the *fruits* of the Spirit as well as the *gifts*. We have many brothers but very few fathers. We need pastors who are worshipers first, and will lead by example so we can follow them as they follow the Lord. Yeshua said in John 5:19 that He *only* did what He saw His Father do. Pastors, please don't tell us to do what you say without being a living example of *how* to do it!

NO COMPLAINTS

I am confident that by now you understand my firm belief that all these wonderful expressions of praise and worship should be placed under the direction of the chief musician or worship leader of the congregation. He or she should be in regular contact and fellowship with the senior pastor or rabbi who gives vision and direction for the house as they carry out that vision for the services.

Remember that none of the instruments or restored expressions mentioned in this book are essentials that we cannot do without. If you don't have an anointed shofar player, tambourine player, dancers, banner and flag ministry, it doesn't mean that your worship will somehow fall short. Be prayerfully patient and the Lord will supply according to His abundance and wisdom.

My friend Pastor Robb Thompson from Chicago said something to me years ago that I will never forget. He said, "Never complain about what you permit!" As leaders, we need to give direction to the areas entrusted to us. I would add this to Pastor Robb's statement: "Never complain about what you have the power and authority to change!" I like that. We need to take responsibility for things, be a man or woman for God, step up to the plate, and hit it out of the park.

We need teaching on praise and worship and some direction from the platform as to what is good and acceptable in the house. As the head goes, so goes the whole body. In other words, if you permit the indiscriminate sounding of shofars and tambourines without any direction, and the free expression of flags, banners and garments of praise, then don't complain about all the confusion and lack of focus during worship. You might also observe that people come noticeably late to service, just as worship is finishing. Training and instruction will produce *skill*; skill will give birth to *freedom*; freedom opens the gates for *joy*; and as we all know, the joy of the Lord is our strength! Sheep need a Shepard, an orchestra needs a conductor, and a house of worship needs someone to lead and direct the worship of God. Pastor, you may not be a musician, but you are the worship leader in your congregation.

CHAPTER 7

THE ROSE OF SHARON

I was preaching in a congregation on the east coast when I said something that absolutely caught me by surprise! "The ministry of *aromatherapy* … it's not just for Catholics anymore!" Hmmm … is it possible that this is an area of worship that we independent, messianic, protestant types have overlooked? The sense of smell, I've been told, is the strongest of all the natural senses. It can stimulate areas of the brain that bring back memories of people, places and events that are stored deep inside the memory banks of the mind. This strong stimulus can also stir the emotions and recall pictures and videos to the main screen of the brain. Now obviously these senses and images can be used for good as in worship, or for the enemy to bring back the pain of the past.

The Lord Himself even made a very specific recipe for the incense that was to be burned in His presence in the tabernacle and the temple. How powerful it would be to link sweet smelling incense and pleasant fragrances with worship and the joy of His presence! Although this special incense was not to be replicated and put into common use, I am thinking that perhaps we might need to reconsider this ministry and its use in our houses of worship today. Not to be paraded where the smoke fills the room and becomes overpowering, but a subtle and gentle fragrance that is present in the sanctuary and becomes associated with worship and the presence of God.

I really do think that our sense of smell in worship should go beyond the cologne or perfume of the person standing next to us. Perhaps this is an ancient element of worship that will be restored to our churches and congregations in the days to come. The burning of incense today has lost some of its special attributes, as it has been associated with the drug culture of the 60s and 70s and the occult. All I am saying is this may be yet another way to say to the Lord, "You are welcome here. We have prepared a place for You to inhabit our praise."

SILENCE IS GOLDEN

Yes, it has been said that silence is golden, but it could also be said that in our contemporary worship services that "silence is the holy 'Selah' that we seldom hear!" Many years ago the prophet Habakkuk declared, "But the Lord is in his holy temple; let all the earth be silent before him" (Hab. 2:20).

Why are we so uneasy with the sounds of silence? Why do we feel the need to fill every moment of our worship services with a song, prayer or declaration? Since prayer and worship are both forms of communication as well as communion with the Lord, then it would make perfect sense that we should give Him an opportunity to speak to us during these times. It occurs to me that listening is also a part of effective communication, and may be the part that we are so lacking!

I recall enjoying one such time during a conference at Word of Life Church in Fort Myers, Florida. After a good time of high praise with dance and banners, shouting, singing and declarations, a holy hush overtook the congregation. Some people stood in reverent awe while others found a place on their knees or lay prostrate before the presence of the Lord. And although there were many children in the room, they did not fuss, fidget or complain. Five minutes turned to fifty and then to seventy-five, and the atmosphere seemed to be supercharged with the glory of the presence of the Lord. Children stood waving banners and flags silently for more than an hour and fifteen minutes! Some people seemed frozen in positions of prayer or praise, and not a human sound was heard the entire time.

When the service concluded there were many testimonies of healing, deliverance and answered prayer. People reported that they had a deep sense of being refreshed and renewed during those minutes, and an unexplainable joy and peace filled many hearts. More than a year later, the people who experienced that visitation were still speaking of the encounter with a wonder and reverence. The Lord *does* speak to His people; are we listening?

TOO OBVIOUS?

It may seem almost too apparent to even state, but when we are quiet, the Lord has an opportunity to speak. Real conversation is never one-sided; it takes two in order to have a relationship with meaningful dialogue. I believe the Lord has much more to say to us corporately; perhaps even more than we may be willing to hear! In Isaiah 65:12 the Lord scolds Israel with these words: " ... I called but you did not answer, I spoke but you did not listen." Yeshua declared in John chapter 4 that the Father was seeking those who would worship Him "in spirit and in truth" (v. 24). In my understanding of true worship, *listening* is just as essential to the act of worship as *bowing*. In both the Greek word *proskineio*, which literally means to "kiss toward," and the Hebrew *shachah*, which means "to bow down," there is an understanding that you will *listen* to the One you are "kissing toward" and "bowing before."

Obviously the quiet and silence can also be taken to an extreme and become something I am not suggesting. In fact, I know of a small denomination that does gather together for meetings and will sit silently in a circle waiting for someone to receive a message or a song to share with the rest of the group. Why do we always seem to be falling off the road into one ditch or another? However, if we *never* experience times of quiet with expectant listening, then I believe we are missing something very special. In John 10:4-5, Yeshua said that His sheep *listen* for His voice, but they will run away from a stranger's voice because they do not recognize it. We need to cultivate a listening ear if we are ever going to be an obedient people!

Isaiah declared, "'Come now, let us reason together,' says the Lord" (Isa. 1:18). Zephaniah tells us that the Lord rejoices over us with singing, (Zeph. 3:17). If we are always the ones speaking and singing, how will we ever hear what the Lord is saying to His people? Not silence for silence sake, but that we are edified, corrected and trained up in righteousness, which is the expressed purpose of the Word of the living God!

If you were to play a thousand different recordings of the song "Days of Elijah" for my sons (and there may well be a thousand different ones by now!), they will pick out my voice every time without fail. Is it because they are such astute musicians, or is it simply because they know their father's voice? The answer is obvious. If we have developed a listening ear as leaders, we will be able to help our people to move past the initial discomfort of corporate quiet "listening" to become worshipers who treasure and recognize the voice of their Father!

WITHOUT A VISION...

We need the voice and understanding of mature, seasoned leaders of worship and praise. Everyone appreciates the young, fresh sounds and enthusiasm of the next generation of God-chasers in our midst, but we must also have the wisdom and experience of our fathers in the sanctuary. It is right that the pastor should select and employ an anointed person with the passion and vision for corporate worship and give them authority to instruct and conduct it under pastoral direction. Certainly the pastor, and the worship leader, if he or she is able, should spend quality time teaching on the different expressions of praise and worship and then give direction for the implementation of them in your house of worship. Direction always brings order, and order brings peace and freedom. When people understand *why* they are doing *what* they are doing, it gives them confidence to step out boldly in their worship of the Lord and leaves little room for a spirit of confusion to operate.

If there is no anointed leader for these different areas of ministry, why not pursue them? Very often, "we have not, because we ask not!" Every time I joined a ministry or a congregation it was because someone invited me! Over the years, several pastors, elders, and board members have asked me to pray about joining their staff or to help them with a problem. There is no harm in asking and pursuing people and their giftings, as long as it is done in a covenantal way. By "covenantal," I simply mean that all conversations are held with the knowledge and agreement of all the parties involved. For instance, if I wish to speak with a brother or sister who is employed by or is attending another congregation, I speak with their pastor before speaking to them directly. I have always followed this pattern when asking people to join this ministry and I can tell you that this is the only way I will operate.

Let me give you a personal example of how this works, as I have now opened up this little can of worms. Greg Shumake is on staff with this ministry primarily as our music director/keyboard player, and travels and ministers with me everywhere I go. Several years ago, before Greg joined our staff, our music director believed he was called to start his own ministry. Suddenly we found ourselves in need of someone just like Greg. Although I had a personal relationship with Greg for more than ten years and could have called him directly, I did not do that. Instead, I found the phone number of his pastor and called him first to discuss the possibility of a change in his church staff as well as Greg's life.

After introducing myself, we talked about many important things at some length. I asked him several questions, including: Do you think that this lifestyle would be good for Greg and his family? How would this affect the church staff, congregation and worship team. Are you comfortable with me approaching Greg to speak about the possibility of a change? I believe Pastor Danny Chambers and I spoke for more than an hour about these things as well as many others. We had never met prior to this conversation and still have not met face-to-face, but because this conversation *did* take place before any offers were made, Pastor Danny and I will always have a good relationship of trust. This is what I mean when I say "covenantal," that everything is done in the light so that fellowship is not broken with our brothers and sisters or the Lord whom we all serve. I just wish I could say that others have acted this way when it came to speaking to men on my staff!

People will come and go, that is a fact of life and ministry. But, *how* they come and go is a matter of covenant and character and is more important to the Lord and *His* reputation than some care to consider. No matter how you've been treated in these areas in the past or what you might think of the leader you need to approach, the covenant is more important than your opinion, period! How we live out our relationships before the world is a very powerful testimony regarding the truth of the gospel that we sing and preach. If we do not honor and respect the brothers and sisters we *can* see, why do we think we are loving the God we *cannot* see?

CHAPTER 8

ORDER OR FREEDOM?

Order and freedom are NOT mutually exclusive! In fact, it is the very instruction and example from the platform that frees the people to express themselves to God. Now, it is entirely possible to so *order* the service that people feel like they are attending a Broadway performance where nothing is expected or permitted from them. We can also have so much "freedom" that no one is certain what is acceptable or who is in charge. Vision will give birth to motion; the motion will demand to be ordered (and possibly staffed), and the order will bring freedom and joy to the house of the Lord.

The Scriptures say, "Where there is no revelation [vision, KJV], the people cast off restraint" (Prov. 29:18). Our services should neither be a free for all where anything goes, or a place where the worship police clamp down on any emotional response to the presence of the Lord. In fact, it is His presence amongst us that sets us apart from all the other "religious" groups in the world! (See Exodus 33:15–16.) He inhabits the praises of His people (Ps. 22:3). In His presence is fullness of joy (Ps. 16:11, KJV). And, the joy of the Lord is our strength (Neh. 8:10, KJV)!

A people of praise are a people of strength. We need to give the house the liberty to praise the Lord of Glory, and to direct the worship in such a way that draws the honor of His presence. May the Lord help us to worship Him with passion, in the beauty of holiness as well as in spirit and in truth.

SPIRIT-LEAD, SPIRIT-FILLED

It should be abundantly clear by now that the presence, power and ministry of the Holy Spirit is absolutely necessary during our times of worship! Even though we are the same people meeting at the same times using many of the same songs, dances, banners and flags, there should be a sense of freshness and life making every service unique. Invite the Holy Spirit to inhabit the praise. Expect the Holy Spirit to energize you and the time you give to Him, and yield to His leading when He does come. There is nothing more fulfilling for a house of worship than to experience the joy of His presence week after week as He leads, guides and speaks to His people. As King David said, "We are his people and the sheep of his pasture" (Ps. 100:3, KJV). If we allow Him, He will lead us beside still waters, guide us into victorious living, train our hands for war, anoint our heads with oil, and bless us until our cups run over the top!

After some thirty plus years of walking with the Lord I still pray what the disciples asked of Yeshua many years ago: "Lord, teach [me] to pray [and teach me how to worship]" (Luke 11:1). In John chapter 4, Yeshua describes the kind of worshiper that the Father seeking: those who "worship the Father in spirit and truth" (v. 23). I want to be that kind of worshiper!

THE GIFTS IN WORSHIP

Before speaking about the gifts and their place in corporate worship, let me simply quote for you here what the apostle Paul wrote to the believers at Corinth some 1,900 or so years ago:

> *Now to each one the manifestation of the Spirit is given for the common good. To one there is given through the Spirit the message of wisdom, to another the message of knowledge by means of the same Spirit, to another faith by the same Spirit, to another gifts of healing by that one Spirit, to another miraculous powers, to another prophecy, to another distinguishing between spirits, to another speaking in different kinds of tongues, and to still another the interpretation of tongues. All these are the work of one and the same Spirit, and he gives them to each one, just as he determines.*
> *(1 CORINTHIANS 12:7–11, EMPHASIS ADDED)*

Now I do realize that "spiritual gifts" is one of those subjects where we have divided ourselves into groups and even denominations with regards to the understanding, use and even the relevancy of these very precious things. And so it is with a certain sense of "fear and trembling" that I approach the subject knowing that some of you will disagree with my premise right up front that these giftings are not only available today but that they are necessary for us to activate and appreciate in these modern times. In fact, I believe that to ignore or refuse a place for these things is to close the door to the Giver of these gifts. Let's take a closer look at what the apostle Paul is saying here by the power and inspiration of the Holy Spirit.

First of all these gifts are given by *Him* in order to manifest *Himself* in our midst. Secondly, they are given to everyone, and thirdly they are given for the common good or for everyone in the commonwealth of God's kingdom! These words alone should cause us to think differently about how we order our worship and what we should be expecting during those special times. It is not my intent in this brief work to thoroughly examine each and every gift of the Spirit and to explain how, when and where they are appropriate to be utilized. Rather, my desire is to encourage the ordered expression of these gifts during our corporate times of praise and worship. (If you, the reader are Pentecostal or Charismatic then what I am saying will be cause for you to wag your head up and down in immediate approval, however if you are a non-charismatic evangelical you may have already found my comments to be outside your experience or practice. I sincerely hope that these few words of encouragement will cause us all to re-examine the "what, why and where" of what is normal in our worship lifestyles.)

Now I suppose that if we all simply kept these gifts to ourselves that all would be well, but it is the public use and display of the gifts that gives us a cause to pause. Then again, if we were all 'self contained' pre-packaged perfection just like Yeshua then there would be no need for the body or for fellowship or most other exercises of the Spirit for that matter. However, we *do* need each other and the benefit that each member supplies!

With that said, I am certain many of us have been in services where the gifts have been present and can probably tell lots of hair-raising stories about the good, the bad and the ugly things we have experienced. My purpose here is not to critique or to criticize, but to encourage the use of God's gifts for the common good of all.

Praying in the Spirit

Praying and singing "in the Spirit," in a "prayer language," or in "an unknown tongue" is without a doubt the most misunderstood and potentially controversial gift in the list Paul gave to the church at Corinth. However, I have personally found this expression to be a tremendous blessing as well as a means to participate in prayer and in worship that can stir our hearts and minds as deep speaks to deep. Not practiced in a voice that is loud and discernable above the others so as to draw attention to oneself, but in a modest way that will edify my own spirit and keep me in a high level of participation with the worship leader and the Lord. Yes, I understand this is an area of confusion and doctrinal separation among denominations, and some groups even go so far as to state that this is not a gift from the Lord, but a deception from the enemy. Other denominations will not allow a person with this gift to hold a position of leadership or responsibility in the church and are instructed they must not use the gift in the congregation.

I am not being critical here but I believe I must speak the truth in love. Paul tells us in 1 Corinthians 14:2 that those who speak in a tongue are speaking to God. He also instructs us that when we do this we are edifying or building ourselves up in our most holy faith, and we utter mysteries with our spirit (vv. 3-4). Now I ask you, who in their right mind wouldn't want to (1) speak to God, (2) utter mysteries, and (3) edify, encourage and build themselves up? Now Paul does go on to say that it is much better if the tongue is interpreted because this edifies the whole congregation (v. 5). Granted, but it is also much better if we are all participating in the praise and worship utilizing the gifts the Lord has given us! And yes, it must all be done decently and in order according to the rest of the direction given us by God for orderly worship.

Since I have opened up another little can of worms here I will go ahead and finish my thoughts on this subject. It has been said that the inauguration of the church took place in Acts 2 (during the Feast of the Lord of Shavuot or Pentecost) in direct fulfillment of the prophet Joel's words in the book that bears his name and the same chapter. Now, if the New Covenant was instituted and confirmed with this gift in Acts 2; and if the engrafting of Gentiles who were validated as authentic occurred by the giving of this gift to Cornelius and his family in Acts 10:45-46; and if we heed the Holy Spirit, speaking through the apostle Paul in 1 Corinthians 14:39, specifically warning us NOT to forbid speaking in tongues, then I think we should simply go with the clear teaching of the Scriptures on this one. It is indeed possible today, as it was in Jesus' day, that there are doctrines of men that have crept in amongst us, which make the clear teachings of the Word of God of no effect. Yes, there are abuses in the operations of some of these things, but there are also abuses in the omission or even the forbidding of these gifts that need to be addressed and corrected as well.

GIFTS AT WORK

The operation of these gifts during worship has played a major role in my life and ministry. I can remember several instances when I received a word of encouragement from the Holy Spirit in an unknown tongue that was then interpreted in song complete with verses that rhymed! Messages from the Holy Spirit can come this way and are a blessing to the congregation. One of the roles of the worship leader is to help prepare a place for the presence and ministry of the Holy Spirit *through* the saints as well as through the leadership. (How this takes place, as well as when and where, are all the responsibility of the pastor and the spiritual leaders of the house.)

I remember so clearly leading worship at a congregational re-treat back in 1982 when our speaker for the night stepped up to the platform and "interrupted the flow" with a prophetic word for my wife and me. He spoke in tongues and then in English with a confidence and a "knowing" that what he was saying came right from the throne of God. It was powerful, encouraging, and it was *a confirming word* that launched me out into full-time music ministry (again!) and the forming of the recording musical group Israel's Hope! Thank you Bob Weiner for being obedient to the Holy Spirit, and thank you Dan Juster for allowing the Lord to have the freedom to speak to His people! That one word changed the course of my life and since that time has had a direct effect on many others as well. These gifts are given by the Holy Spirit and are intended to be used for the good of the body as well as to be a sign for the "not yet believers" in our midst.

Let me just step aside for a moment here to explain what I believe about New Covenant prophesy and words of knowledge or words of wisdom. An Old Covenant prophet had some pretty strict guidelines placed on him for the public use of his gift. Namely, get it right first time, every time, or take a very long and pain-ful nap under a very heavy pile of stones! Obviously, we do not hold New Covenant prophets to this kind of scrutiny for several reasons; one very good reason is that murder will get you twenty years to life! Prophecy and prophets under the New Covenant are using the God-breathed words of the Scriptures to tell-forth truth, and to forecast future events that have been revealed to them by the Spirit and the Word. They are not writing scripture as Jeremiah, Daniel and Isaiah.

Personal prophecy can be a blessing sent by heaven to encourage you and yes, it can also be a diversion or a distraction sent by the enemy to derail you. This is where discernment and the inner witness of the same Spirit of God with your spirit will tell you where and from whom this 'word' is coming. Is that last statement clear to you? Don't simply receive anything anyone says to you; rather test it by the Spirit and the Word of God to see if it is from the Lord or from another source. If it is from God, then you will have an inner witness to that fact, and it will line up with what you know the Lord has been saying to your heart and teaching you personally. The Lord has built a fail-safe system into His plan in order to keep His children from running after every wind of doctrine and deceit that comes along; He's called the Holy Spirit!

Ten years after that word came to me from Bob Weiner, Israel's Hope had fulfilled our calling and season and I found myself on staff at a large independent church in the south suburbs of Chicago. Pastor Robb Thompson and I had been friends for many years and Israel's Hope had ministered at Midwest Christian Center many times. Although I moved to be the worship leader and an associate pastor, we all knew this was not a forever thing, but it was for the next season of our lives. Well, wouldn't you know that during one of the very first services at my new assignment that our dear and trusted friend Bobbie Jean Merck was the invited speaker. I lead the worship and sat down to hear what the Lord was going to say through this anointed vessel. The very first thing out of her mouth was a prophetic word for my family and me. I was having a déjà vu moment when she opened her mouth and began to speak in tongues and then interpreted her own words in English. "I see planes and boats and trains in your future, and lots of them," she began. I instantly knew that what she was saying had come right from the throne room of God, and although I spent the next five years on staff there in Chicago we all knew what was in store. And so when the phone call came from Don Moen and Michael Coleman at Integrity Music in the summer of 1994, I knew the answer would be "yes." So it was off to Israel to record "Shalom Jerusalem," and then lots more trains, boats and planes ever since.

I love the gifts of the Spirit, and the sanctuary is the perfect place for them to be utilized to edify, encourage and admonish the saints as well as to demonstrate to the visitors that we serve a living, powerful God! It would be one thing if we worshiped the Baals, sticks and stones with no ears, no voice and no power, but we don't!! We worship the God of Abraham, Isaac and Jacob; the God of Moses and of David, the God of the Prophets and the Apostles, and the God of our Lord and Savior Yeshua the Messiah (Eph. 1:3). He does have ears that hear, a voice to speak, and a passion to lead and direct us as we worship. Our people are not interested in nicely packaged and predictable services; they are hungry for an encounter with the God they worship!

I could go on here, but this is not a treatise on the Holy Spirit and His work amongst us. He deserves another whole book of His own! I also understand that His work and gifts is a subject that is used by the enemy to divide the body today. It is very sad to me that the One who was sent to unite us, to teach us about all things and to lead us into all the truth has been so misunderstood on so many important issues. King David declared in Psalm 133:1, "Behold, how good and how pleasant it is For brethren to dwell together in unity!" (NKJV). He goes on to say that it is like oil that is poured out on the head and flows down over the garments, and then he finishes with this remarkable statement: "For *there* the LORD commanded the blessing, even life for evermore" (v. 3, KJV)! Where is the "there" that David wrote about? It is wherever the people of God dwell together in unity! Not uniformity—rubber-stamped, glassy-eyed robots that simply do what they are told—but passionate lovers of God and His presence. And of course there is the prayer of Yeshua Himself in John 17:11 when He prays, "Father ... may they be one as We are" (NKJV). Real worship softens the heart, breaks down barriers and sends spiritual pride running for its life. When we worship together, when we bow down together, when we kiss toward the throne together we become the "one new man" of Ephesians 2:14. Help us Lord!

CHAPTER 9

A WORD TO PASTORS

Pastors, the Lord has given you a great privilege as well as a great responsibility. I have had the blessing as well as the opportunity to work alongside some of the most anointed leaders today, and I want my words here to reflect my deep admiration and gratitude for the difficult task you perform every day. I am not called to be your teacher or your armchair critic, but I do hope that my words will be an encouragement that will spur you on to love and good deeds!

The people are crying out today for leaders with a heart after God who will be fathers that demonstrate how to worship the Lord as well as being teachers who explain why we worship. I have noticed one common trait in all the pastors I have had the honor of serving, and it is this: shepherds never follow their flocks; they always lead them. If you are frequently absent during the worship, or you never participate in the praise, what do you think the people understand about your actions? You are teaching them by example that this time and these expressions are simply not important to a mature believer. How long will the children listen to a father who continually says to them, "Do what I say, not what I do"?

It is sad to me when I find myself in a position where I have to minister over the top of the front row in order to be effective in the rest of the house. The people who inhabit the front row of seats are generally the staff or elders, guest ministers and their spouses. Experience has taught me that there can be a lot of talking, greeting, studying, Bible reading, and just general activity going on in these seats that can not only be distracting, but they can also be very confusing for the worship leader and the congregation. Because of all the movement, questions arise in the worship leader's mind that challenges his or her effectiveness and even anointing. This is neither healthy nor helpful. I guarantee that no pastor/teacher I have ever met would allow such things to go on while they are teaching. So then, why should our attitude be any different while we are supposed to be worshiping the God of the universe?

The apostle Paul told the early believers to, "Follow my example, as I follow the example of Christ" (1 Cor. 11:1). In other words, pray with me, worship with me, praise the Lord with me, and I will teach you by example how the Lord desires to be worshiped and adored. Why do so many of our American pastors assign the prayer and praise leading of the congregation to other leaders and then are noticeably absent when these vital life-giving ministries of the body are taking place? Paul also told us to be imitators of God, to speak to one another with psalms, hymns and spiritual songs. Do your people ever see you so excited about God that you jump and dance before Him in the sanctuary? Have they ever heard you so caught up in praise that you prophesied as easily as drinking water or breathing the air? Have you ever joined the dancers like King David or waved a flag in the presence of the Lord?

Pastor, your personal expressions of praise and worship are the most powerful tools you have to demonstrate to your church what is good and pleasing to the Lord of lords. They will learn more from your life of worship than you could ever teach them from the pulpit! "Well, I'm just not a very demonstrative person." Then why do you insist that the people "amen" loudly and often while you are teaching or preaching? "Clap your hands, all you peoples! Shout to God with the voice of triumph!" (Ps. 47:1, NKJV). "Lift up your hands in the sanctuary, And bless the Lord" (Ps. 134:2, NKJV). I could go on, but the point is clear. These are not suggestions or even invitations; they are exhortations that expect a response! None of us, or very few of us I should say, grew up in homes where these expressions of worship were practiced on a daily basis. I understand that, but this is certainly no excuse for the mature leaders of the house of God not to lead!

Some time ago I shared a weekend of worship and teaching with Dr. David Reagan of Lion and Lamb Ministries. He is a very distinguished and revered teacher, who has, how shall I put it, celebrated his 50th birthday for many years now! His words were strong and full of truth, but more than that, I will never forget his response in worship to the presence of God. At one point, he grabbed a flag of Israel and waved it over the congregation with all his might, then he handed the flag to someone close at hand and joined the children as they danced before the Lord to the song "Shouts of Joy."

Other pastors/teachers who instruct by the example of their lives as well as their words come to mind. I think of my dear friend

Pastor Emeritus Don Finto of Belmont Church in Nashville, Pastor Jack Hayford of Church on the Way in Van Nuys, California, and Dr. Judson Cornwall (who has now gone on to be with the Lord). We desperately need more fathers like these wonderful men of God! How do they remain fresh, relevant and sought out after all these years? I would suggest that one secret to their longevity and success is the simple fact that they are passionate, wholehearted worshipers who are unashamed of their Lord and King!

Our young men and women are crying out to be discipled, to be shepherded, to be taught by the example of true fathers who are mature lovers of God. I have personally found my life enriched and refreshed when I happened to observe a maturing believer who was lost in a passionate worship of his Creator. Pastor, I encourage you to be a David in your house of worship. If you will teach the congregation by the example of your life as well as what you say, you will release an anointing in your people to be the kind of worshipers the Father is seeking today! The body of Messiah is in desperate need of fathers in worship as well as fathers in the Word!

PATIENCE: MORE THAN A VIRTUE

Be patient in the process of building your worship team and staff. The pain of removing the wrong person far outweighs the pressure of waiting for the right person to appear! Gifted people with anointing are not as scarce as you might imagine. When I minister in worship conferences I meet many people with anointing and potential that have yet to be tapped. In fact, I met Connie Wright at a worship dance conference some twenty-five years ago when she was just an interested student. Today she leads Messiah Dance Company, a troupe of more than twenty-five dancers who travel with us all over the world!

Send your worship leaders and team members to conferences of worship and they will make the connections and relationships with dancers, musicians, banner creators, and more. These conferences are also great opportunities for your people to catch a fresh vision of who they are and what they have been created to do.

Here is another thought for you. You can hire someone with the gifts you need for a season until they duplicate themselves in your people who will eventually take over the position. I have done this myself in the critical ministry of the audio department. I hired a professional soundman from the company who installed the new system in our sanctuary. He came to services every week to run the soundboard until our own people were trained and capable of running the sound on their own. I know of churches that have hired key leaders to fill important positions for them until the right person showed up. Could this be done with the dance, the banners and flags, and with the shofar and other instruments? Absolutely. It might mean that as a pastor you will have to change your mind about some things. I have heard some leaders say that they will never hire people to play in the worship team or run the soundboard. That's fine; but you may need to pray for exceptional patience and grace for you and the congregation while you are raising up these people from within!

A WORD TO WORSHIP LEADERS

If you are a worship leader in a church, messianic congregation or synagogue, you have been given a great privilege as well as a tremendous responsibility. The people in your congregation are looking to you to help them connect with God in a significant and meaningful way.

Do you remember the first time you went to a worship service where the people were doing things you might not be comfortable with like clapping their hands, dancing and singing with all their hearts? Do you remember how awkward and "out of place" you may have felt? People are no different today. Your visitors are looking for a place to worship God that is safe as well as provoking. The quality of worship that comes from the platform as well as the confidence you display as a seasoned leader will go a long way toward bridging the gap between their lives, your congregation and heaven.

I think of a worship leader as a kind of tour guide. You are charged with taking people "in the spirit" to places that may be new, uncharted waters for them. They want to know that you are going where you have been before and can help them avoid the dangers as well as experience the joys of corporate worship. Imagine going to Africa and hiring a guide to take you and your family out into the bush to see the lions and tigers and buffalo. You enter an office where a shingle has been hung declaring that this fellow is an experienced guide who will show you the sites and bring you all back in the same physical shape you left. As you enter, you hear the frantic voice of the man you hired on the phone asking all kinds of questions. He wants to know where the animals can be seen; what are the best routes to get there; he asks what kind of vehicle is best and where to find lunch for a group of tourists that won't kill them. Are you really going to trust this man, much less pay him, to take you out to dangerous places with your family and bring you back? I seriously doubt it! Here are two statements that I believe are absolutely true: (1) you cannot give what you don't possess, and (2) you cannot lead others where you have never been.

I would like to encourage you with some things that have really worked well for me as well as many other leaders I have spoken with around the world. First, spend as much time in prayer and intimate worship with your team as you do rehearsing the music. I have yet to find a better or more effective way to build a close-knit team than this! You will find very quickly that your prayer and worship together will carry over into the sanctuary and the corporate times of worship. The Lord will not only use that time to weave your hearts together but He will speak to you and show you what He wants to do in you and the congregation.

Secondly, if you haven't already, please acquire the skills necessary to be successful in your position. I am still amazed at the number of worship leaders I encounter today who do not read music or play an instrument. If "worship leader" is the place you believe the Lord has called you to stand, you would do well to have the tools necessary to communicate effectively and efficiently with your musicians. Why struggle to build a house with hand tools when there are brand new power tools available? In just a few hours time you can learn the basics of how to read music and to use some of the terminology that will make you fluent in the language of music.

Thirdly, be sensitive to the needs, likes and dislikes of the pastor you serve and his worship life. Interview him on a regular basis and discover the songs that really help him connect with the Spirit of God. Plan your song list around what he believes the Lord is saying to your congregation and particularly for individual services. Be careful not to resist his instructions and direction and certainly be careful how you portray him to the people you are leading. Remember that the pastor was called by God to lead the congregation, and then the pastor called you to assist him in this ministry. You have been called alongside the pastor to help the people hear the voice of God and experience His manifest goodness and presence, not to replace him!

What I am speaking about here is the spirit of Joshua verses the spirit of Aaron. When Moses went up the mountain to meet with God, Joshua stayed in the tent to pray and support his pastor/leader. Aaron, on the other hand, was afraid of the people and fell into terrible sin by taking the headship in Moses' absence, following the people into idolatry.

SHEPHERDS OF WORSHIP

I am certain that by now you know where I stand on many different issues. Yes, the application and administration of all these elements of worship can be messy, and yes there can be abuse and misuse of prophecy and the vocal gifts of the Spirit, but I am not willing to throw out the gifts with the bathwater! In the same way, I won't stop driving my car simply because some people use them for crime and drive-by shootings! It seems to me that we welcome the King into our midst but then we duct tape His mouth and tie His hands and feet and tell Him to sit in the back while we run through our program. Where is the fear of the Lord? We need to know before whom we stand, and who it is that we came to worship. Only then will we give Him the honor and place that belongs to Him alone.

The worship leader can be like a plowman who turns over the soil of the hearts of men and waits for the seeds of the Word of God to be delivered and planted. At other times, you are a gardener who waters the growing plant or plucks the locusts that have come to eat the leaves or devour the fruit. The worship leader is a pastor or shepherd of worship. This is the reason that at times the roles of pastor and worship leader can get confused in the minds of the people. The leader of worship can become very precious to the heart and life of the congregation, but he must always remember that he is not the pastor and that these sheep really belong to the Lord! Worship leader, be very careful that you are directing the affections of the people toward the Lover of their souls and that you are not looking to receive their affection and appreciation as a reward for your hard work!

You are called to be a Kenaniah in the house of the Lord. (See 1 Chronicles 15:22.) He was appointed over the singers and choirs for the carrying of the Ark up to Jerusalem because he was skilled, but David was still the ultimate leader of worship in Israel. You are the worship leader because you are anointed and skilled, but the pastor is still David in the house!

FATHERS AND MOTHERS

The relationship you build with your pastor is just as important to fulfilling your role as a worship leader as the relationships you build with those who are a part of the worship team and the congregation. I see the relationship between a pastor and worship leader mirroring that of a husband and wife. The pastor is the father of the house who has been called and anointed by God to lead the home and protect it from any and all who would try to do any harm. Your role is similar to the wife who would support and honor the husband but plays a different, yet significant role in the life of the congregation. The anointings are very different and yet they are both essential if there is to be a happy, healthy environment for the "kids." Just as the husband and wife learn how to defer to the anointing on each other, a pastor and worship leader will also need to learn when and how to defer to the anointing in each other's lives.

I am sure you have been in a home or two where there is constant friction and a sort of competition between mom and dad for control of the house and the children. This is neither comfortable nor healthy for anyone in that home. Mom is more than a housekeeper and Dad is more than the guy who "brings home the bacon." There are many other functions that each of them performs in order to keep the home running efficiently and peacefully.

As a worship leader, never contradict or work against the decisions or intentions of your pastor/rabbi. Ask him what you are doing that he likes, and ask him what are some things you could do to improve, or what changes need to happen. Listen carefully and implement everything he tells you to the best of your ability. Remember, you are not the pastor; you may even have the title of worship pastor, but there is only one father in any house.

CHANGES

"OK," you say, "but what if my pastor is not a 'worshiper'? What if I only have twelve minutes at each service to bring down the glory? What if he doesn't want dancing, banners and flags; am I in the wrong place at the wrong time?" Well, maybe you *are* in the wrong house, or just maybe the Lord wants to use you to bring about some changes right where you are. If He does, He will make the changes in His way and in His time. The only real question for you to ask is, "Lord, is this where you want me for this season of my life?" The answer to this question is the one that trumps all the other questions and queries! Get an answer to this question and the others will all find their place in time.

Here's another word of advice for you. David was a worship leader in the House of Saul Ministries. It was a wonderful congregation with lots of people and very exciting services. The victories were frequent and profound until one day Pastor Saul heard the worship team practicing their newest hit song, "Saul has slain his thousands, and David his tens of thousands!" (1 Sam. 18:7). It had a great beat, kickin' instrumentation with a shofar introduction, and the people were catching on to the new lyrics without a video presentation! Yeah baby, this was the next "Days of Elijah" for sure. Then it all went south. Why, what happened? Who's to blame? Here's the simple answer: pride stepped in to sing the chorus and along with it came envy, strife, and every evil thing! The point here is this: be a team player, keep your flesh in check, don't take more to yourself than is right for you, worship the Lord and He will take care of your future.

Flesh will only give birth to more flesh; it can't help it. The Lord of Creation set a law into motion in Genesis chapter 1, which states that everything will produce after its own kind, and your flesh is not exempt by any means. I would like to recommend a great little book to you here that has meant so much to so many people for the past twenty years. It is called *A Tale of Three Kings* by Gene Edwards and can be purchased through this ministry in our Web-store at www.wilburministries.com. I believe you will find a great deal of revelation in those pages that will help you see and understand some deep things with regard to relationships and walking in the anointing.

WALKING IT OUT

The first and best way to begin to see changes come about in your congregation is to believe for them in prayer. If the Lord can turn the hearts of mighty kings, He can surely change the heart of a pastor! I love the story of how Smith Wigglesworth came to faith through the constant selfless love and support of his dear wife. One night she came home from a church meeting past the time she told Smith to expect her. He was so upset with her actions that before he went to bed that night he locked her out of the house and would not let her in. All night she slept on the porch without any covers or pillow. In the morning when Smith opened the door to allow her back into the house she said, "Good morning dear, what would you like for breakfast?" If you are believing for some changes and favor in your house of worship, I would suggest that the very last way they will come is through a critical, nagging, fault-finding spirit! Your attitude will not only determine your altitude now, but it will also play a major role in determining your future!

Another way to see changes come about in your congregation is to invite ministries that operate in these areas of worship with excellence. Once your pastor and the congregation have a great experience with an anointed guest, it will open their hearts and minds to want some of that at home every week. Remember how you eat an elephant…one bite at a time! Be a bridge and not a wall; be a humble person who is quick to listen, slow to speak and slow to become angry, and you will have favor with the Lord as well as men!

IN THE BEGINNING

The year was 1981 and I had just left Bloomington, Indiana where

I was born again, married my wife, Luanne, and had our first son, Nathan. It was there that I had been discipled by Jerry Williams and traveled with our contemporary gospel group "Harvest" for more than four years. Although I had been classically trained and had a wonderful background in theatre, music and performance, I had NO idea how to lead a congregation in praise and worship. Our little messianic congregation (fifty people), called Beth Messiah, was nestled in an old WWII neighborhood of Rockville, Maryland and was just beginning to grow in the area of messianic praise. One day, my new friend Keith Intrater, who was also an elder at BMC said to me, "Paul, you should lead worship." I immediately responded with, "Oh no, I couldn't do that!" Well, why not? I had the background, musical training and experience…but did I have the anointing? I think this was the question that was really nagging at me when my friend made that statement. This really is the question that begs for an answer but can only be satisfied when put to the test. In other words, the proof of the pudding is in the eating! Skills can be acquired with training, experience can be gained over time with patience, but anointing, that can only come from the Holy Spirit. This was, without a doubt, the one request that occupied my prayers after I agreed to "try" being the worship leader for the congregation.

If there is anything that the body of Messiah needs in any generation it is this: anointed leadership! I learned early on that anointing carried with it a quality called responsibility. I also learned that anointing was attainable by more than one means. In other words, the anointing is certainly a gift of the Holy Spirit, but the anointing can also be transferred! Remember Elijah and Elisha, David and Solomon, Moses and Joshua, and Asaph the Levite musician and his sons? Yeshua breathed on the disciples and told them to receive the anointing, or Spirit of God. He said in the Sermon on the Mount," If you, then, though you are evil, know how to give good gifts to your children, how much more will your Father in heaven give good gifts to those who ask him!" (Matt. 7:11, emphasis added). I love that phrase: "How much more?" More than a great voice, much more than incredible musical skill and so much more than decades of experience is the anointing of the Lord. Now let me back up a few verses and quote him again: "Ask and it will be given to you ... For everyone who asks receives ..." (Matt.7:7, 8).

Now, am I really saying that all anyone has to do in order to become an anointed worship leader is to "ask"? Is that what I am saying? ABSOLUTELY NOT! What I *am* saying is written for us there in 1 John 2:20 that states that all of us have received "an anointing from the Holy One." Now, what *kind* of anointing? What it is there for and how I put it into motion is now my responsibility to discover! In fact, verse 27 of that same chapter tells us "his anointing teaches [us] about all things," including what the anointing is in our lives to accomplish for the King!

Here are a few practical suggestions for some of you. Avail yourself of the wonderful opportunities to be involved with some great conferences during the year. There is a very large and popular Worship Institute every year in Dallas; Hillsong hosts a great one in Australia; and Integrity Music holds several conferences around the country and the world. There is always something to be gained from the knowledge and experience of these seasoned and anointed leaders. Take some time to travel and experience the leadership of others you admire in their home worship settings. Ask them questions and have them lay their hands on you and transfer some of that anointing into your life! There are also some very good publications out there that can be of assistance to you: "Kairos" and "Worship Leader" are among some of the best that I know.

I am frequently asked to pray for worship leaders after a concert or service. It is not an imposition to me, but it is a privilege to sow something good into the lives of others. I have talked with many experienced worshipers who feel the same way I do. Don Moen, Ron Kenoly, and Paul Baloche all consider it an honor to share with and to pray for others who are leading the praises and the "praisers" of God. Remember, you have not if you ask not (James 4:2)...so ask, seek and knock!

AND SO, IN CLOSING

There should always be a house for true worship, and for true worshipers to express their adoration to the Lord. There should always be room for the dance, for the extravagant worship, for the banners and the flags, for the prophetic, for the garments and for the instruments, but they all need to be submitted to the leadership of the house. As my good friend Pastor Russell Johnson of Lancaster, Ohio would put it, "Be willing to be stretched without fracturing the bones."

Individual expression that dominates, distracts our attention or affection, or infringes on the expression of corporate worship is always out of order. When the personal worship of an individual competes with the corporate worship of the house, it needs to be corrected. The beauty of a symphony is that each individual player in an orchestra submits to the authority of the maestro. No matter how great their anointing or skill as an individual may be, they will discipline that gift to conform to the blueprint of the music, the intention of the composer, and the direction of the conductor.

The Scriptures so clearly state in Psalm 133: "Behold how good and how pleasant it is For brethren [brothers and sisters!] to dwell together [worship together] in unity! ... For there the Lord commanded the blessing" (vv. 1, 3, NKJV). Where does the Lord command His blessing? It is in the place where unity abides. King David never said that the Lord inhabits the passion of His people, or even the best intentions of His people, but He *does* inhabit their praises (Ps. 22:3). Our God is not the author of rebellion or chaos (1 Cor. 14:33). Those fruits are a certain sign of the presence of another spirit. But the fruit of His presence is order, self-control, and the full expression of the kingdom of God.

This order liberates a house of worship to focus their affections on the Lord and to take control of the atmosphere. There is no room here for strange fire, Asherah poles or the prophets of Baal! We are in a glorious time of the revival of worship in all of its expressions. "Taste and see that the Lord is good" (Ps. 34:8) and let all things be done decently and in order. "May he send you help from the sanctuary" (Ps. 20:2), and may there be Order in the Courts of the Lord!

ENDORSEMENTS

An 'on time' work that I believe will allow the new wine to be poured out into new wine skins. There has been much prophecy recently concerning the restructuring and re-aligning of the third day church. I believe God has given Paul Wilbur a major truth in *Order in the Courts* that must be released to the body of Christ in order to accomplish this great latter day move of God. Jesus is coming back for a bride that is washed and cleansed by the Word of God. Paul's many years of experience and spiritually keen insights will release correction, direction and vision to the covenant community of believers in their primary call to be worshipers. I know that every true worshiper who is longing to draw closer to God will be extremely blessed and encouraged by this masterpiece. I know that I was.

Bishop Gaspar Anastasi
Word of Life Church
Fort Myers, FL.
Freeport, N.Y.

"Paul is to praise and worship what Starbucks is to coffee!

Pastor Larry Tomczak
Atlanta, Ga

"Savor these words of insight, influence, wit and wisdom. Order in the Courts is an expression of God's heart and His invitation to passionate, strategic and purposeful worship directly into the Throne Room of the King of Kings. Paul Wilbur's voice as a father, mentor, friend and visionary is vital for this and the next generation."

Pastor Peter Hirsch
Southlake, TX

BIOGRAPHY

The world's opera stages were the ambition of a determined young man named Paul Wilbur. A passion for the arts, music, and teaching took him from undergraduate school in Cleveland, Ohio across the Atlantic to study in Milan, Italy. There he was instructed in vocal technique, Italian, and high-opera by some of Europe's most skilled mentors.

"By the time I had returned from Italy the direction of my life had been pretty well set in stone," Paul says. "The life of Richard Tucker had become a pattern to success that I wished to emulate. Here was a Jewish man, who was one of the world's most revered operatic icons, and who also honored his religious tradition by singing under the domed roofs of the world's synagogues." All of this was about to change.

"I was pursuing a Master's Degree in vocal music at Indiana University, and the things that normally attract a young man were also attractive to me: music, my friends, and girls. As I pursued relationships, inevitably two things happened: I asked girls out for a date, they invited me to church." The writing was on the wall.

"It was like I wore a t-shirt that said, 'Please … somebody take me to church.'" Well, it was during one of those "church dates" that Paul encountered Jerry Williams, a young man from West Texas, whose testimony and friendship would change his life forever.

"I was completely taken by Jerry's love and passion for God. From the very first time I saw him 'perform,' I understood that he was not singing about God, rather he was singing to Him. It was as if he actually knew the God I sang about at temple: the One whose voice I longed to hear."

This was all new to Paul. Being raised in the home of a Jewish father and a Baptist mother, he grew up attending a variety of churches. While in college he joined The Temple in downtown Cleveland, singing in the sanctuary choir. But now, he was being impacted for the very first time by the manifest presence of God.

This experience, along with powerful teaching from the Scriptures, continued to draw Paul week by week. He joined a Bible study in his graduate dorm and became hungry for anything that could teach him about the God of the Bible.

One Sunday the church announced that anyone who would like a free meal would be paired with a church family. Paul signed up, but then had second thoughts.

"I was picturing this grandma and grandpa, and my payment for eating their dinner was going to be hours of conversation sitting in a room with quilts over our laps looking at pictures of their grandchildren," he recalled thinking.

But try as he might, Paul could not get out of the commitment. When he arrived at the house, he was completely overcome to see the young man whose music had touched him so deeply several months earlier. It was just a few weeks later on a fishing trip to Tennessee that Jerry introduced Paul to his Messiah. The day was March 26, 1977.

"In the next several weeks I began to understand the truth of 2 Corinthians 5:17, which says, 'If anyone is in Christ, he is a new creation.'"

Together with their friend Ed Kerr they formed the popular contemporary Christian group "Harvest." They traveled and ministered together, and recorded several albums on the Benson Record label, Milk & Honey.

"What an incredible time this was for my life," Paul says. "But the call to bring the gospel back to the Jewish community grew stronger and stronger in my heart." After nearly five years, Paul yielded to this call and moved his small family to the Washington DC area, and a fledgling messianic congregation.

"For two years I worked odd jobs and found part-time work to pay the bills until the Lord brought together three Jewish men and called them "Israel's Hope." We traveled and ministered together for more than eight years recording several albums on the Maranatha! Record label."

MUSIC, TEACHING, AND MERCY MINISTRY

Today Paul's ministry is as worldwide as his music. "God's grace is truly amazing," Paul says, "as we have ministered in more than thirty nations, recorded in three languages, and have witnessed thousands set free by Messiah-empowered worship and praise."

One of the aspects of this ministry that may not be apparent at first glance is Paul's commitment to the marriage of music, ministry, and acts of mercy. "As we travel to third world nations we seek to bring a larger expression of the kingdom of God in a practical way. Dr. Paul Williams staffs free medical clinics to minister to the needs of the poor; Paul Cuny brings MarketPlace Ministry to the business community; Messiah Company brings the beauty of movement to worship, while Integrity Worship artists stir the hearts to joyful song."

Paul sees his calling is to build bridges of reconciliation between the church and the Jewish community. His latest recording for Integrity, "The Watchman," is a stirring call to the body of Christ worldwide to take up their place on the walls of their lives, congregations, cities, and nations—to be faithful, prayerful, and watchful during what he calls "this most prophetic hour."

"The Watchman" was recorded live on Yom Kippur at Cornerstone Church in San Antonio with Pastor John Hagee. "Yom Kippur, or the Day of Atonement," he explains, "was the one day of the year that the high priest was allowed to come before the presence of God, and only with blood, making atonement for himself and all Israel. I believe this recording will carry that anointing in a very special way and will sweep many into the kingdom of God."

You can reach us, send prayer requests, purchase product, and discover more about Wilbur Ministries buy visiting www.wilbur-ministries.com